Following God for YOUNG ADULTS

DISMANTLED

An Honest Look at Some of Our Biggest Fears

A STUDENT DEVOTIONAL GUIDE
by
David Rhodes & Chad Norris

Advancing the Ministries of the Gospel
AMG *Publishers*
God's Word to you is our biggest calling
CHATTANOOGA, TENNESSEE

Following God:
DISMANTLED Student Devotional Guide

Published by AMG Publishers.

ISBN:0-89957-734-2

First printing: June 2003
Edited by: Robert Neely and Rick Steele
Graphic design: Jeff Belk at ImageWright Marketing and Design, Chattanooga, TN
Cover design: Jeff Belk at ImageWright Marketing and Design

Wayfarer Ministries
Box 201
1735 John B. White Sr. Boulevard
Suite 9
Spartanburg, SC 29301-5462
864-587-4985

Printed in Canada

08 07 06 05 04 03 -T- 6 5 4 3 2
web sites: www.wayfarerministries.org   www.amgpublishers.com

To Emma and Sam:

May you grow up in love and not fear!

Table of Contents

DISMANTLED

Fear. . . . It is one small word, but it has an enormous impact. Nothing in today's society seems to drive people like this emotion. We make our decisions because of fear. We hide behind it. We are motivated by it. Sometimes we even find comfort in it, because it is all we know. But many of us discover that the road fear leads us down is a dead end, full of shallow promises, empty hopes, and unrealized dreams. In the middle of our battles with fear, we find that our lives have been turned upside down and inside out without us even knowing. We find ourselves journeying to places we never intended to go or, even worse, not journeying at all.

This book is written out of our own battles with this paralyzing emotion. The specific fears we address here have at times been barriers to our walks with God. We have spent a lot of time dealing with fear in our own lives and have felt its stinging reality. We have been trapped at times. At other times, we have traveled in directions we are not proud of because we were scared to face fear head-on. But God in his mercy has shown us a different way. It is a road less traveled but a beautiful road indeed. It's a road that leads directly to the shelter of the Almighty, where fear has no power over us. We have found that shelter in his love, acceptance and tenderness. Our prayer is that this book will help you begin to walk down that road as well. Many saints throughout the ages have abandoned the road of fear and said yes to love – God's love. It really is true that "Perfect love drives out fear."

Chad Norris and David Rhodes

...on using this Tips... devotional book

This student devotional book is intended to help you learn how to overcome your fears and begin to walk down the road of following God in spite of your fears.

Some of you are working through this study on your own, and some of you are going through this study in a group. Either way, this book is designed to take some of the truths of key characters of the Bible and help you apply these truths to your daily life. Our hope is that, if you've gone through the devotions in the week leading up to your group time, you will be able to share your thoughts with the group and build on the things you learned during the week during that time. If you are going through this study on your own, we hope that you will take some time to enter into discussions with your friends, family, and ministers about the things you are learning.

The book is divided into eight lessons with the purpose of allowing the reader to do one lesson per week for eight weeks. Though the first lesson serves as an introduction to the study, each lesson following centers on a Bible character who dealt with the issue of fear. There are five devotional readings for each week's lesson. Although we have divided the devotions according to the five-day schedule, feel free to create your own schedule for completing your study.

Recognizing that there is no perfect structure for time alone with God, we have tried to produce devotions that are both varied and consistent. This book provides stories, questions, illustrations, background information, charts, and other tools to help illuminate the featured Scripture for each day and encourage and challenge your view of following God.

Finally, at the end of each week, there is a notes page, which we hope you will use to take notes during your group session if you are going through *Dismantled* with others or to journal your own personal highlights from the week if you are going through the study on your own.

We believe this study will help you grow in your understanding of fear, and we hope that you will have fun in the process. Let the journey begin.

DISMANTLED

NO FEAR

the surprising
answer to fear

hidden truth
about fear

Have you ever awakened in the middle of the night afraid? Most of us have. For some, it happens every once in a while. For others, it is a nightly ritual.

Little boys and girls often have trouble sleeping through the night. They think the boogeyman is out to get them. Or they believe a monster lives under their bed. Or they're convinced someone is staring through their window. And every now and then, when the nightmares are a little too real and the night is a little too long, they can't stay in their own beds any longer. What do they do? They get out of bed and run to the safety of their parents' bedroom.

When I was young, the scariest person in the world to me was Jack Nicholson. I saw *The Shining* at a very young age, and it scarred me for life. There were many nights when I was sure he knew exactly where I lived and was coming to get me. Unfortunately for me, the scariest night came at an age when I was trying to keep my fears under control. After all, there is a point when it is no longer acceptable to run to your parents' bedroom (like age 27 or so). That night, I was caught between my fear of Jack Nicholson and my pride that I was grown up enough to handle my fears myself. As I paced nervously around the house, I tried to talk myself out of the cowardly act of fleeing to my parents' room.

But as I gave myself a go-get-'em pep talk that would make a football coach jealous, the floor beneath my feet began to creak. Just as I noticed that I was making a lot of noise, my dad heard it and got up to see what was going on. I was in an awkward situation. How could I explain pacing around the house at 2:30 in the morning without looking like a scared little kid? As my dad came out of his room, I ducked beside his door to hide. I decided to act cool, calm and collected, like nothing was going on. My dad opened the door to his room, and I stepped out and said, "Hey, how's it going?"

My dad was so startled he nearly jumped through the roof. For more than a few minutes after that, there were two scared guys nervously pacing the floor.

■ Describe the time in your life when you felt the most afraid.

_____

_____

_____

_____

■ How did you handle that fear?

_____

_____

_____

_____

We live in a terrorized society. Reminders of the September 11 attacks and their aftermath surround us. A color-coded terror alert system is now part of our everyday existence, and the threat of war is more of a reality than ever in many of our lives. When you combine this environment with the commonplace fears of things such as rejection, failure, and insignificance, it is no wonder we often live on the defensive.

Many of us don't realize how living in fear paralyzes, constricts and enslaves us. More importantly, living this way becomes a barrier to embracing the purpose of God in our lives. Plus, the isolation fear creates give it even more power over us.

The hidden truth about fear is that everyone's afraid of something. I was afraid of Jack Nicholson. My dad was afraid of my middle-of-the-night surprise. As we begin our journey into _Dismantled_, we must start with the truth that we are not alone in our fear. While we wear masks that cover fear well, a minor crisis reveals how fearful we really are. Thankfully, the Bible does not leave us to face our fears alone. God invites us, by studying the lives of countless characters with cowardly tendencies, to come into his bedroom and find the peace our souls long for.

Fill in the blanks:

Psalm 34:4 says, "I sought the LORD, and he
_____ me; he _____ me from all my
_____."

■ Do you seek the Lord when you are confronted
   with fear? If so, how so?

_____

_____

■ How do you feel when you think about fear?
   (Check all that apply)

    ❑ paralyzed   ❑ scared
    ❑ in control   ❑ surrendered
    ❑ hopeless   ❑ alone
    ❑ calm   ❑ trapped

Psalm 34 is David's prayer from a time when he had to run for his life, first from Saul and then from the Philistines. The only way David escaped was by pretending to be insane. In this psalm, David tells of God's work in his life. God freed David from the stranglehold of fear, and David's prayer invites us to a similar encounter with God. As he says in verse 8, "Taste and see that the LORD is good." This week, we begin to journey toward being freed from fear as David was. We pray that by the end of this study we will be able to testify to the same truth David did. The Lord is good.

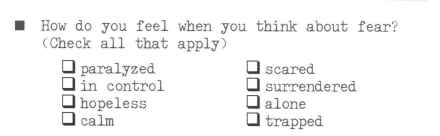
prayer exercise:

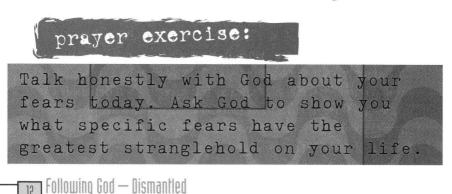
Talk honestly with God about your fears today. Ask God to show you what specific fears have the greatest stranglehold on your life.

when fear
keeps us from God's best

Numbers 13

Those of us who play sports know there is no day like game day. We wake up easily, anxious for the opportunity to play. We treat our bodies differently. We drink lots of water. We eat pasta for added energy. When we see our teammates, we slap hands and make sure everyone's focused. If we see our opponents, we pop off a little trash talk to stoke the emotional fires. Throughout the day, we try to concentrate on other tasks, but the game has our full attention. No matter how much we try to distract ourselves, the game comes racing to the front of our mind.

Finally, the time comes to go to the locker room to prepare for the game. We meet our teammates and put on our uniforms and equipment. As we run onto the field or court, the smells of freshly cut grass or industrial floor cleaner remind us that other people have been preparing for the game as well. As we warm up, look at the lights and see the crowd filing in, we know our moment is coming. The butterflies in our stomachs flutter faster and faster. Finally, the time comes, the whistle sounds and the game begins.

You never know how people will play come game time. You may have seen them in practice, but playing in a game is different. As a coach, I've noticed that there are two types of players on game day: gamers and non-gamers.

Gamers turn their level of play up a notch when the game begins. They practice well, but they are at their best on game day. They may not be perfect, but when they make mistakes, they recover twice as quickly. At the end of the game, they all but have to be carried off the field because they've given their all. A gamer is someone who wants the ball when the game hangs in the balance. They see the opportunity to win, and they go for it.

Non-gamers are just the opposite. No matter how well they practice, a non-gamer's level of play goes down once the game begins. Non-gamers go into a shell because they are so afraid of making a mistake. When they do make mistakes, they hang their heads and sulk as the game passes them by. After the game, non-gamers have plenty of energy. And don't even think about giving non-gamers the ball when the game is on the line. They don't want the responsibility. In fact, they're praying the ball doesn't come their way.

Read Numbers 13

■ After reading this chapter, how would you characterize the children of Israel?

❑ gamers

❑ non-gamers

What kept Israel from God's best?

_____

_____

_____

_____

The difference between gamers and non-gamers is that when everything is on the line, the gamer chooses to risk, while the non-gamer is paralyzed by fear. Numbers 13 is the story of game day for the children of Israel. God promised to lead the Israelites into the Promised Land and give them possession of it. In this story, Israel stood teetering on the edge of the promise as they heard what the twelve spies had seen. Two spies, the gamers, said the land was just like God said it would be, that with his help they could take possession of it. The other ten spies, the non-gamers, talked about the giants in the land and were paralyzed by their fear. The Israelites accepted the word of the ten non-gamers, and, as a result, an entire generation perished in the desert outside of the land of milk and honey God had for them.

■ How should Israel have acted?

❑ believe the ten spies and gone away in fear

❑ believe Caleb and Joshua but not act accordingly

❑ believe the ten spies but trust God anyway

❑ believe Caleb and Joshua and follow God as they did

■ Has there ever been a time when fear kept you from God's best in your life? Explain.

_____

_____

_____

_____

_____

_____

Sadly, the story of Numbers 13 often recurs in the lives of God's children today. How many times in our spiritual lives do we settle for the comfort of staying where we are instead of following where God is leading us? We act like spiritual non-gamers and miss many God-sized opportunities in our lives. One of fear's great strangleholds is that it keeps us from doing anything, making us satisfied to stay in the comfort or pain we know instead of venturing into the seeming unknown with God.

prayer exercise:

Use today's prayer time to ask God to reveal to you how you have been living your life. Have you been a spiritual gamer, or has fear kept you from pursuing God's best? Take some time to reflect on your past and ask the Holy Spirit to help you evaluate yourself honestly. Check the box that applies with you. Then talk to God about the answer to the question on the next page.

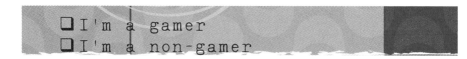

❏ I'm a gamer
❏ I'm a non-gamer

If you are a gamer, what has motivated you to overcome fear in your life?

_____

_____

_____

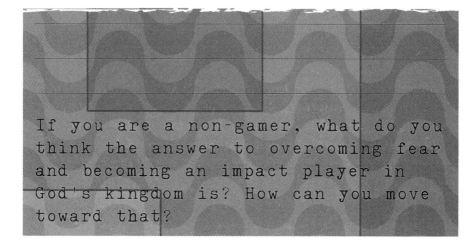

If you are a non-gamer, what do you think the answer to overcoming fear and becoming an impact player in God's kingdom is? How can you move toward that?

knowing
what to do with fear

1 Peter 5:7

Some people love to bear their own burdens. Dr. George McCauslin was one of these people. George was an outstanding YMCA director. But at one time, as he led a YMCA near Pittsburgh, Pennsylvania, things were not going well at all. Membership was down, money was scarce and staff problems were rampant. George was so depressed, anxious and worried over the situation that it took over his life. Before he knew it, he found himself working eighty-five hours a week. Even when he was at home, he worried about the troubles at the YMCA. It got so bad he could hardly sleep at night.

George went to a therapist, who told him he was on the edge of a nervous breakdown. On the therapist's advice, George took an afternoon off and went to the woods to think and pray. After a short walk, he sat down under a tree and started to relax and reflect for the first time in months. He decided to let go of the burdens he had been carrying. He took out a notepad and wrote God a letter. It read, "Dear God, today I hereby resign as general manager of the universe. Love, George." After months of trying, George discovered he couldn't be God. He could only be George. (from Thomas Tewell, "The Weight of the World," *Preaching Today* [1995].)

■ Do you have the tendency to carry your own burdens?

❑ yes
❑ no

If so, how?

_____

_____

_____

_____

■ What truth about life did George McCauslin discover?

_____

_____

_____

_____

Read 1 Peter 5:7

What fears do you think the people Peter wrote to faced?

_____

_____

_____

What did Peter tell these people to do with their fears, cares, and anxieties?

_____

_____

What does this tell us about what we should do with these things?

_____

_____

_____

_____

Everyone goes through difficult periods and rough seasons in the Christian journey. When we are overwhelmed by stress and anxiety and fear, we have to remember we are not alone. Christians throughout the centuries have faced difficult situations and have overcome them through the power and provision of God. The people to whom Peter wrote this letter were some of these overcomers. They faced brutal condemnation from their government for proclaiming the name of Jesus Christ. Many even lost their lives for what they believed in. They knew what fear was! Peter wrote to tell them they did not have to carry their own burdens. They could give them to God.

This verse contains a simple but powerful truth: we were not created to carry our own burdens. God wants his people to cast their cares onto him. He wants to lighten our loads if we will only give our baggage to him.

Many people agree with the command to "cast all your anxiety on him." But many of us don't know how to do that. How does a person overcome by fear, anxiety, depression and stress give it over to God? George McCauslin gives us a great picture. He wrote a letter of resignation. He decided he could no longer handle his worries on his own. This is a form of confession we need to emulate. God is waiting for us to admit we can't handle our own cares. God loves it when his people are desperate for him. Are you? Do you need to confess that you can't manage your fears on your own? Go to God and tell him how you feel.

What are some burdens you need to give to the Lord?

_____

_____

_____

_____

_____

Say the following prayer out loud: "Father, I need you right now. I confess to you that I can't bear my burdens anymore. I want to give you these to you. I want to let you be God in my life. Right now I give you my fears of _____. (It may be one or many. God wants to take them all.) Lord, I thank you for promising never to leave me. I surrender all of my burdens to you. Teach me how to walk in this way. I love you. In the strong name of Jesus I pray, Amen."

why
fearing God is good

Psalm
111:10

So far this week, we have talked about how everyone's afraid, how fear can keep us from God's best in our lives and how we need to learn to cast our anxieties on God. Today we take a timeout to talk about how fear can be good.

I have a miniature schnauzer named Otis who has an unlimited amount of energy and feistiness. When I bought Otis as a Valentine's Day gift for my wife, I had visions of a sweet, precious, submissive, gentle, caring, cuddly, obedient dog. But that vision was pretty distorted. Over the past year, God has taught me a lot about patience through Otis. It has taken a lot of time and effort to get Otis to be obedient and submissive. Trying to housetrain him was brutal. He had no idea why he had to stay in his kennel all day, and he hated every second of it. He barked, howled, and cried in an effort to persuade us to let him out. However, we didn't let him out, because we knew we had to break him and show him who was in control.

As time goes on, Otis is gradually becoming the dog I knew he could be and is growing into a pretty obedient and submissive canine companion. I think he realizes that my wife and I are always going to take care of him. We are not going to leave him. He has learned to trust us. Now he goes into his kennel and sleeps all the way through the night.

Read Psalm 111:10

Fill in the blanks:
Psalm 111:10 says, "The _____ of the LORD is the beginning of _____; all who follow his precepts have good _____. To him belongs eternal _____."

The New Living Translation has a great take on this verse: "Reverence for the LORD is the foundation of true wisdom. The rewards of wisdom come to all who obey him. Praise his name forever!" The key words we should focus on here are reverence and obey. This verse makes it very clear that we are supposed to fear one entity: The Lord.

The fear or reverence the Bible speaks of is by no means the same as being scared. Not at all. We are to be a group of people who honor and respect the Lord with our lives. This reverence should lead to obedience. The Bible is very clear that the fear of the Lord is the beginning of wisdom.

■ What do you think it means to fear the Lord?

_____

_____

_____

Do you fear the Lord?
  ❑ yes
  ❑ no

Why or why not?

_____

_____

_____

To give God reverence is to abandon your own pride and honor God as he deserves. It means acknowledging what you are not and what God is. Reverence for the Lord says, "Father, you are absolutely worthy of my surrender to you. I exalt and glorify you above all others. You are God, and I am not. I give my life to you."

If we want to reverently fear the Lord and be obedient to him, we must be people who take seriously what it means to submit to his authority. We all have fears we need to address. The first step in dealing with those fears is living with appropriate fear or reverence of the Lord. Let us obey him by surrendering our lives. He will never leave us or forsake us. Through our fears, he will draw us to himself.

■ Why do you think God places such a large
emphasis on people submitting to Him?

_____

_____

_____

■ What are some ways in which you need to be
more obedient to Him?

_____

_____

_____

prayer exercise:

Spend some time being quiet before
the Lord. You may want to ask God
what areas of your life you need to
hand over to him. Ask yourself some
tough questions. Do you fear the
Lord? Are you living in obedience
to him? Are you holding some things
from him that he wants you to
release? Take your time and be
honest with the Father.

a surprising
answer to fear

1 John
4:16-18

■ What do you think is the answer to fear?
- ☐ courage
- ☐ love
- ☐ both courage and love

Have you ever watched a child jump off a diving board for the first time? The child's reaction is almost always the same. Fear constricts tightly around his small, floatie-framed body. The youngster walks to the edge only to stand there frozen between the possibility of fun and the risk of the unknown. Many times, the child stands at the end of the board for twenty to thirty minutes debating in his mind just what move to make next. Parents standing on the side of the pool watch him struggle with this seemingly insurmountable challenge. They encourage their child to jump and reassure him that everything will be OK. Still, the child is held fast by fear, because courage alone is not enough to conquer this powerful fear.

More often than not, something happens that changes everything for the child. Just when you think he will never leap from the diving board, his father jumps into the water, opens his arms and calls, "Jump! I'll catch you!" Delight and peace race to the child's face. A few short moments later, the child has jumped in the water and waddled back to diving board, where he stands and pleads, "Let's do it again, Daddy!" What courage alone could not overcome, love did.

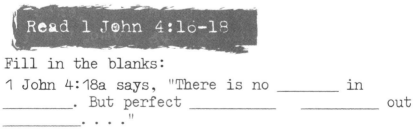
Read 1 John 4:16-18

Fill in the blanks:
1 John 4:18a says, "There is no _____ in _____. But perfect _____ _____ out _____. . . ."

Most of the time, when we think about the answer to fear in our lives, we think of courage. Courage is "the state or quality of mind or spirit that enables one to face danger with self-possession, confidence and resolution." Courage enables us to overcome fear by disregarding it, thus allowing us to live in spite of fear. Many times throughout the Bible, courage is shown doing just that. But the message of 1 John 4:18 is that we have another help in our battle against fear. John says that love is the answer to fear. While courage merely helps us overcome fear, love drives fear out.

It is surprising to think of love as an answer to fear. In fact, at first the two seem only distantly connected. But it's love that spurs a child to jump off the diving board. It's love that gives a scared child peace in his parents' bedroom. John reminds us that love helps drive fear out of our lives as well. What courage many times cannot do, love can.

■ Does it surprise you to think about love as an answer to fear in your life?

❏ yes

❏ no

■ What are some situations in your life where God has demonstrated love's power to drive out fear?

_____

_____

_____

_____

Over the next few weeks, we will journey through some of the fears many of us face everyday. Many times these fears keep us from following God. This is not a new problem. Thankfully, the Bible is honest about its God-followers. Throughout its pages, many of the people we consider heroes of the faith struggled through their own fears just like we do. The truth is that the Bible is full of cowards who were transformed by the power of the love of God. Through the lives of Esther, Jeremiah, Moses, Elijah, Hagar and Joshua, we will identify the fears that affect our lives and experience together the way God loved these people through their fears.

prayer exercise:

Get quiet before God. Ask him to show you someone in your circle of influence who needs to know that he or she is loved. Ask God for ways you can show that person that you love him or her and that God loves him or her. Pray and thank God for his great love that allows us to love each other and follow him regardless of the fears we face.

_____

_____

_____

_____

_____

_____

_____

_____

_____

_____

_____

_____

_____

This page is designed to give you space to take notes during your "Dismantled" group session or to journal your reflections on the highlights of this week's study.

DISMANTLED

FEAR OF DEATH

esther: hope in
the face of death

face to face
with death

My first experience with death came when I was five years old. My grandfather, who was one of my favorite people in the world, passed away. I had such a hard time grasping the reality of his death. It was so tough to have him around one day and then gone the next. I remember asking my parents, "What is Papa doing with Jesus? Why did he have to die?" These are difficult questions. Death is not a fun experience.

As I grew and began to understand my grandfather's death, I came face to face with my own mortality. I realized that one day I would die too. This is a frightening concept for many people. It bothered me for a long, long time, until God showed me what he has to say about death.

Throughout my life, I have experienced the deaths of loved ones and friends. Every time death comes close to me, I am reminded that one day I, too, will pass away. But now God has given me a peace about that. The God I worship will take me into his arms when I physically die.

■ Why do you think so many people fear death?

_____

_____

_____

_____

■ When you think about dying, what do you think about?

_____

_____

_____

_____

Esther was queen of Persia, and a man named Haman had it out for the Jews who lived there. He asked the king to let him destroy the Jews, and the king agreed. What neither Haman nor the king knew was that Esther was a Jew. In his sovereignty, God had put Esther in position to approach the king and ask him to save the Jews.

But this was no easy task for Esther. Anyone who approached the king uninvited, including the queen, could be put to death. If Esther went to the king, she was basically signing her own death warrant. To fight for her people, Esther had to come face to face with her fear of death. If she was going to do what God had put her in position to do, Esther had to come to the end of herself.

■ What would you have done in Esther's place?

❑ ignore Mordecai and hide her Jewish heritage

❑ write a letter to the king asking for help

❑ run for your life

❑ do what Mordecai asked

It is not natural to enjoy thinking about your own death. But it is possible by the grace of God to overcome the fear of death. One of the ways that God helps us with this fear is by calling us to come to the end of ourselves and give up being so self-centered. The courage to face death comes when we humble ourselves before God and say, "My life is not my own."

The fear of death is really a surrender issue. Esther could have simply hidden the fact that she was a Jew. But while she would have survived, countless others would have been killed. This week, as we talk about the fear of death, we will face the same surrender issue Esther faced. At the end of the week, we will see how Esther responded.

Be honest with the Father. Tell him how you struggle with the fear of death. Ask him to show you what he has to say about it. Be still before the Lord. Ask the Holy Spirit to guide you to truth that will help you deal with this fear. Tell the Father that you want to cast this fear on him. He will take it if you let him.

death wasn't
God's idea

John
11:1-37

Most of us acknowledge the reality of death, but we see it as very distant from us. Death happens to old people in retirement homes or to sixty-year-old men who need to lose a little weight or to refugees in third-world countries. But sometimes, death becomes an all-too-present reality. Just a few days before I wrote this devotion, a commuter plane leaving Charlotte, North Carolina, crashed at the terminal, killing all twenty-one people on board. The flight, bound for my hometown in upstate South Carolina, is one that I have been on several times. I'm sure that when I board a plane for Alabama in a few weeks, the crash will conjure up vivid images in my mind.

The day the plane crashed was surreal. Most of the people in our office have been aboard commuter planes from Charlotte to the upstate more than once, so it was no surprise when the phone rang from time to time from people checking to make sure we were all OK. But as we watched the footage on CNN, our hearts went out to those whose relatives would not be able to answer those questions as we did. How do you balance a God who is in control of everything with the horror and uncertainty of death?

The truth is that these questions of God and death are painfully real to people across our world this very day. Just a few weeks ago, one of my best friends had to bury his father. When death happens to someone close to us, it always seems to catch us off guard. And the older we get, the more frequent the questions become. As I listened to my friend describe the shocking news of his father's death and the pain in his heart, I reached for something to say to bring him comfort. But sometimes there are no easy answers.

■ What questions about God does death bring to your mind? (Check all that apply.)

❑ How could a good God let this happen?

❑ Is God really in control?

❑ Does God really care?

❑ How does God feel about death?

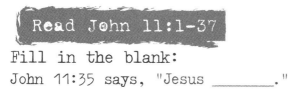

Fill in the blank:
John 11:35 says, "Jesus _____."

Yesterday, we saw Esther face the fear of death in her life. While many of us live without facing this fear on a daily basis, at some point in our lives, it will become all too present. Esther feared both for her own life and for the lives of her people. If she had not faced this fear, she would have missed a divine opportunity.

As we turn our focus from Esther to ourselves, we start with the question, "How does God feel about death?" Some of us wrestle with this question because of tragedy in our lives. Others encounter this question in theory as they try to explain a God who is in control to unbelieving friends. It is questions like this one that leave far too many of us paralyzed in our journey of following God. While there are no simple answers to this dilemma, we get a great picture of God's heart in John 11.

Jesus was ministering when he got word that his friend Lazarus was deathly ill. But when he reached Lazarus' sisters Mary and Martha, Jesus was told he was too late. Jesus arrived in the midst of mourning. Death had taken its toll.

Jesus knew the power he was about to unleash on this scene. But while it would be easy to jump to the end of the story, John takes time to show Jesus' heart. Jesus went to Lazarus' grave, and then, John says simply, "**Jesus wept.**"

When I look at this story, I wonder why Jesus cried. Did he miss Lazarus? Was he trying to fit in with the rest of the mourners? Was he heartbroken by their pain? Was he disturbed by the devastating consequences of man's sin? I cannot say for certain, but I know this: death was never God's idea. God is the creator of life. Jesus wept because he saw and felt firsthand the pain and agony that man's choice to sin brought upon the world.

■ How does it help you to know that death was never God's intention or idea?

_____

_____

_____

- What comfort do you take in Jesus' pain as he cried over his friend Lazarus?

_____

_____

_____

- How does seeing God's heart help you experience his love as you face the fear of death in your life?

_____

_____

_____

_____

prayer exercise:

Ask God to bring to your mind anyone in your circle of influence who is going through a hard time because of the death of someone close to him or her. Even if the death occurred a while ago, that person may still be dealing with it. Ask God how he can use you to show his heart to this person. Spend some time in silence and ask God to show you how to pray for that person and what you may need to do to encourage him or her.

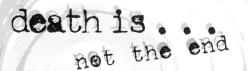

death is . . .
not the end

Let's pick up the story of Jesus and Lazarus where we left off yesterday. Lazarus had died, and Jesus showed us the heart of God as he wept over his friend. Now, we get a glimpse of God's answer to death in our lives.

Read John 11:38-43

■ What truth about himself does Jesus demonstrate in this passage?

_____

_____

_____

_____

_____

Fill in the blanks:

John 11:25-26 says, "Jesus said to her, 'I am the _____ and the _____. He who _____ in me will _____, even though he _____; and whoever lives and believes in me will never _____. Do you _____ this?

■ What does Jesus mean in these verses?

❑ We will never die a physical death if we believe in him.

❑ Even though we may die physically, we will not die spiritually if we believe in him.

- **What does this story tell us about the power of God?**
    - ❑ God has power over death.
    - ❑ Death has power over God.

It seems like everyone today has something to say about life. The Raelian cult says human cloning will let us live forever. Health experts say exercising and eating right can add years to our lives. Maybe Elvis Presley and 2Pac have it figured out, since they keep selling millions of CDs long after their deaths.

I was in my dentist's office not too long ago, and the lady cleaning my teeth began to explain the importance of flossing. I'm not a huge fan of the dentist. I don't like the way they poke at your teeth and gums with sharp metal objects. I hate when they put fluoride that tastes like sand in your mouth. Most of all, I hate the way they floss your teeth, digging into your gums so much that it seems they don't believe they've done their job until your mouth is full of blood. But the hygienist told me, "If you floss, you can add six years to your life!" To hear a truth like that while I was in utter agony made the whole flossing experience worthwhile.

After I left the dentist and thought back, though, I wasn't sure about the correlation between flossing and long life. I called my dad later that day and casually brought it up in conversation, and I was astonished when he said he had heard the same thing on the news a few days earlier. After I hung up the phone, I began wondering just how this flossing thing worked. If I tried to cross the street and got hit by a bus, would someone check my gums? Would the ambulance driver take special confidence in the fact that I flossed? "He's a flosser! He's going to make it!" Somehow, I'm not convinced that flossing's promise of a longer life has the lasting impact I'm looking for.

In John 11, Jesus gave his take on life. He said that he is the resurrection and the life and that not even physical death can hinder the resurrection work he brings to those who believe in him. Jesus is not saying that those who believe in him will never face physical death. Jesus himself tasted this reality in a gruesome way. But Jesus does promise that we can face death without fear if we have given him our lives. Just as Lazarus experienced Jesus' resurrection power, we will experience resurrection one day.

The promise of Christianity is the promise of *life*, and this promise of life is available to *all* who believe in Jesus as their Savior and Lord. Death is not the last word for those who follow Christ. We can face death because the last word in our lives is *resurrection*.

Read 1 Thessalonians 4:13-18

How does Paul describe the hope we have in Christ?

_____

_____

_____

prayer exercise:

Spend some time praying for people in your life who need to know that Jesus is the resurrection and the life. To identify these people, use the three ovals on the opposite page. In the innermost oval, write the names of family members or friends who need to know Christ. In the second oval, write the names of co-workers, teammates and peers who need to know Christ. In the outside oval, write the names of acquaintances and classmates who need to know Christ. Pray for these people as you write their names down. If you're having trouble coming up with names, ask God to help you identify people around you who need him. Ask God to show you how you can live in a way that shows these people the life Jesus offers to those who believe in him.

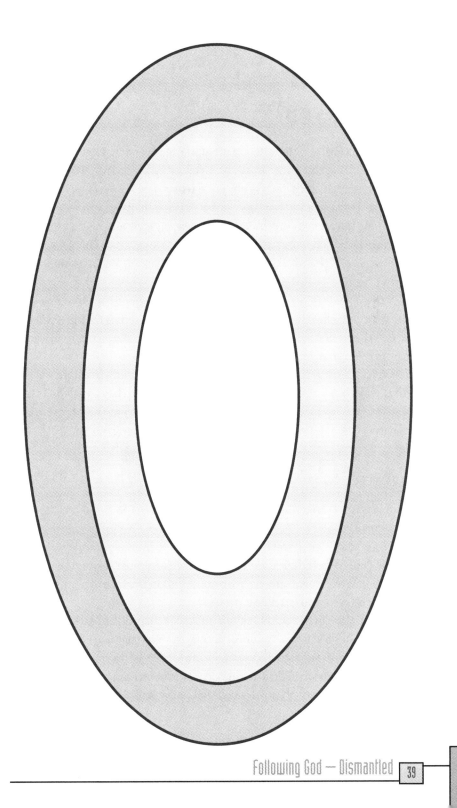

to die...
is gain

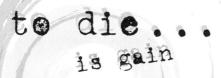

I have two close friends who are missionaries overseas. They serve the Lord in the dangerous environment of a country where the government hates Christianity. Each day as they go to work, they know danger surrounds them. Not too long ago, I received an e-mail from them that showed me how dangerous their situation really is. Some missionaries who served with the same organization a few hours away from them were killed because of their beliefs. It was a tragedy that shocked missionaries like my friends around the world.

My friends wrestled with the fear of death. Most of us can't imagine what it must be like to live in such a dangerous situation. But as they grieved the death of their fellow laborers, my friends came to a conclusion: To live is Christ and to die is gain.

I wonder if I would be so bold. My two friends continue to inspire me with their choice to give their lives to God. They know they could die, but it doesn't bother them. They don't fear death. They have put their trust in God and agreed with the apostle Paul. If they die, it is nothing but gain!

Read Philippians 1:19-26

Paul was no stranger to the thought of death. As a matter of fact, he faced it on a regular basis. He was preaching a dangerous message in a dangerous place. One thing that stands out to me in this passage is the attitude Paul had. He didn't fear death; in fact, he almost seemed to welcome it. Why? How could he be so confident in the face of something that strikes terror into so many others?

The answer lies in the one about whom Paul preached. Paul gave up everything after his dramatic conversion. Everything that had been so important to him had withered away in comparison to his relationship with the living Christ. So when death came close to him on many occasions, it didn't terrorize him. Like Esther, Paul decided that to live is Christ and to die is gain.

■ Can you identify and agree with Paul's
statement that to live is Christ and to die
is gain?

    ❑ yes

    ❑ no

■ How do you think Paul got to the place where
he could say this?

_____

_____

_____

_____

■ What will it take for you to get to that
place if you are not already there?

_____

_____

_____

_____

Fill in the blanks:

Philippians 1:23 says, "I am torn between the
two: I desire to _____ and be with
_____, which is _____ by _____."

■ Why do so many people fear something Paul
says is better than what we know now?

_____

_____

_____

To get to the point where we can say, "To live is Christ and to die is gain," we must abandon ourselves. You have to be unselfish to make this statement. It's so easy to be self-centered and obsessed about our own lives. But Jesus calls us to abandon this life and enter a life that puts him and others before ourselves. This is what my missionary friends have done. They have placed things far more important than themselves in front of their own lives, knowing that this decision could lead to death.

At the bottom of this struggle is a liberating truth: So what? What if I died serving God? If something happened to you or me and we died, those of us who are born again would enter a place that completely trumps where we are now. This is great news. No wonder Paul said to death, "Bring it on." For the believer, with death comes the presence of God. Focus on his love. Focus on his presence. This will drive out your fear.

prayer exercise:

Read the following paragraph that my missionary friends wrote after their colleagues were killed. Use it to be honest with God about your own fear of death. Make their prayer your prayer today.

Today we have once again been reminded of the costs we bear for our calling to be Christ's ambassadors around the globe. Today, we grieve the loss of our colleagues who paid the ultimate price for their faith in Christ.

We are faced with a difficult question: Is Jesus worth it? Is Jesus worth risking our lives for? Is it worth living for Jesus among people who hate Christians? For those of us who have been called to serve the Lord in hostile environments, we are faced with this question every day of our lives. Is Jesus really worth it? If we didn't think that he was, we would have packed our bags a long time ago. The apostle Paul said, "To live is Christ, and to die is gain." As we travel through this earthly journey, we will indeed live for Christ. And when God does call us home to be with him in eternity, we will have gained everything.

Today, our three beloved colleagues were no doubt greeted by their Creator, along with all the other saints of our Christian heritage, with a thunderous applause as they left this finite world and entered into Paradise. May their lives and their sacrifice be an example for us all. May we live as boldly as they did, and may we discover in our own hearts that Jesus Christ, the Messiah, is indeed worth every minute of it.

dead woman
walking

■ What do you think it means to die to yourself?

_____

_____

_____

■ Have you ever considered yourself dead to the world, your flesh and your own desires?
  ❑ yes
  ❑ no

Explain that situation.

_____

_____

_____

_____

Fill in the blanks:

Galatians 2:20 says, "I have been crucified with _____ and I no longer _____, but Christ _____ in me."

What does this verse mean?

_____

_____

_____

Not long ago, a huge ice storm hit my hometown in South Carolina. Ice storms are more vicious than snowstorms. They wreak havoc, especially with trees and power lines. This particular storm left more than a million homes without power. When it began, my wife and I heard loud crashing noises outside all night long. It was frightening.

We didn't figure out what had happened until the next morning. We have a lot of trees in our yard, and the ice that accumulated on the branches caused them to snap off. Our yard was a complete mess. Huge branches that had once hung thirty or forty feet up on massive oak trees were lying all over the place on the ground.

As I drove around over the next few days, I saw huge limbs down everywhere. But not every tree had lost its branches. I wondered why some trees lost limbs while others did not. After asking a few friends about it, we figured out that trees that had not yet shed their leaves had the most trouble. Huge branches had fallen off these trees and taken chunks of the trunk with them. But the trees that had shed their leaves were far less damaged. Only the trees without leaves, the trees that looked dead, were able to live through the storm. I learned then there is great power in shedding leaves.

Just as trees need to shed their leaves to survive storms, we must be willing to let go of things in our lives to survive when storms of a figurative nature come our way. But it's not always easy to let go. Esther faced this difficult choice.

Read Esther 4:15-16

This week, we've had to come to grips with our own mortality, just as Esther did. God called her to a task that was very dangerous. She had to approach the king of Persia to ask for help even though there was a law that said she could be killed for doing so. A female like Esther was even more likely to be killed in that situation.

Esther weighed her options. She knew that by doing what God was asking her to do, she could lose her life. I'm sure she struggled with this decision, but the conclusion she came to was amazing: "If I perish, I perish."

How could Esther be so bold? What enabled her to say this? I believe God brought Esther to a place where she realized that, although the thought of death was frightening, God would be with her. If she died, he would bring her into his heavenly presence.

On a scale of one to ten, how strong is your fear of death?

◄──── 1 ═══════════ 5 ═══════════ 10 ►

(lowest)   (highest)

All of us struggle with the fear of death to some degree. It's normal to be afraid of death. We've learned this week death was not God's idea. As we've seen, God has not left us to deal with this fear on our own. God can bring resurrection out of death. He asks us to die to ourselves so that we can discover what real life in him is all about. Erwin McManus said, "God has called us to go where only dead men can go, and too many of us are trying to find ways to go there while we're still alive." But we've learned that to live is Christ and to die is gain. We don't have to wonder about what is going to happen to us. As he always does, God answers our fear.

Death ushers us into God's presence forever. I can't think of anything better. Satan loves to feed us lies, and his lies about death lead to fear. But the truth is that the God we serve and worship here and now will be there with his arms open wide when we die. Praise God! We don't need to fear death. Let us stand with Esther and say, "If I perish, I perish."

prayer exercise:

Say the following prayer out loud: Father, sometimes it is so easy to believe lies. It is easy to believe the lie that I have to be afraid of dying. Help me align myself with the truth that you will never leave or forsake me, that you will welcome me into your arms because I have trusted in your son for salvation. Lord, I praise you for being one who drives away my fears.

_____

_____

_____

_____

_____

_____

_____

_____

_____

_____

_____

_____

_____

This page is designed to give you space to take notes during your "Dismantled" group session or to journal your reflections on the highlights of this week's study.

DISMANTLED

FEAR OF SUFFERING

jeremiah:
something worth
suffering for

face to face
with suffering

There is a shocking phenomenon in sports today. It's not the salaries baseball stars are making. It's not the rush of high schoolers to the NBA. It's the growth of something some people don't even consider a sport: stock-car racing. NASCAR is one of the fastest growing sports in America, even though those of us who don't like it believe the only one hundred thousand people who actually do like it must go to every race. Sunday after Sunday, fans flock to the racetrack to cheer their favorite drivers as they cut opponents off, bump them or even spin them out in an effort to cross the finish line first. The drivers race the final laps with reckless abandon and pent-up frustration accumulated over the previous four hundred some miles. The race car driver's goal is to distance himself from everything and everyone behind him.

There is another vehicle that drives at high rates of speed. It's called an ambulance. Armed with sirens and a skilled driver, the ambulance weaves in and out of traffic racing toward its own finish line. Knowing that every second counts, the ambulance races with reckless abandon. The ambulance driver's goal is to close the gap between the driver and the hospital so that the patient will survive the ordeal.

Each of us can be defined by one of these vehicles. Some of us are like race cars, living life for our own interests, consumed with getting ahead in the world and trying to distance ourselves from the troubles behind us to do so. Others of us live under a different reality. Like the ambulance, we use our resources not to distance ourselves but to drive into trouble to bring restoration to a world in desperate need of help.

Following God leads us to live differently than we naturally would. While it is easy to seek our own comfort, God often calls us to a way of life that forsakes comfort and increases our chances of suffering. Probably the greatest example of a person in the Bible who suffered immensely as a result of following God is the prophet Jeremiah. God called Jeremiah at an early age to bring the word of the Lord to the nation of Judah. Judah had forsaken God, so God sent Jeremiah to bring a message of judgment. As you can imagine, Jeremiah's message didn't sit well with the people of Judah.

Throughout his ministry, Jeremiah was faced with the choice of following God and increasing his chances of suffering or following comfort and avoiding God's call.

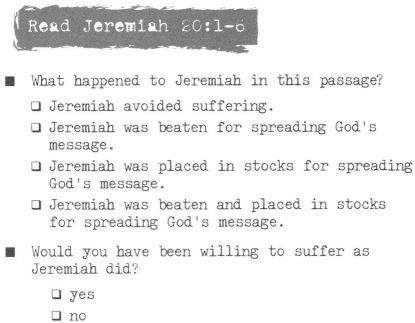

Read Jeremiah 20:1-6

■ What happened to Jeremiah in this passage?

❑ Jeremiah avoided suffering.

❑ Jeremiah was beaten for spreading God's message.

❑ Jeremiah was placed in stocks for spreading God's message.

❑ Jeremiah was beaten and placed in stocks for spreading God's message.

■ Would you have been willing to suffer as Jeremiah did?

❑ yes

❑ no

Suffering comes in many different shapes and sizes. Sometimes it is physical, as it was for Jeremiah in this passage. Other times it comes in other forms such as rejection or ridicule. Jeremiah experienced all of these things. Think about the things that Jeremiah went through as he followed God:

■ He was beaten with forty lashes.

■ He was placed in stocks so he could be publicly ridiculed.

■ He was the subject of death threats.

■ He was falsely accused as a traitor.

■ He was imprisoned.

■ He was thrown into a pit three times.

■ He was the laughingstock of a nation.

■ A scroll that recorded what he said was destroyed.

■ He was commanded by God to remain single to symbolize the barrenness of the land.

■ He was called a false prophet by other prophets.

Very few of us living for God today face the magnitude of suffering that Jeremiah did. But it's amazing how quickly the possibility of suffering sends us running away from God. Too many times, we are so consumed with comfort that we disregard or subtly change God's message for the world and calling on our lives. This week, we are going to address the fear of suffering and ask God to love us through this fear.

prayer exercise:

Do some research to learn about people around the world who are suffering for the cause of Christ. Web sites like www.persecutedchurch.org and www.christianpersecution.info can help you with this. Pray for Christians around the world who are suffering from persecution. Then take some time to evaluate your own life. Are you a race car driver who distances yourself from others and the possibility of suffering, or are you an ambulance racing toward others despite an increased chance of suffering? Ask the Holy Spirit to show you the reality about your life as you reflect.

honest
with God

New Year's Day is a time for recommitment. Each January, health clubs are brimming with people who have decided to turn over a new leaf. For the past few years, I have been one of those people. After making a New Year's resolution to work out a few times, I now realize how big a chore it is. So last year, when I made another resolution to get in shape, I started slow to make sure I wouldn't give up my quest for personal fitness.

There was one day, however, when my fitness campaign hit a snag. I had been working out and trying to eat right for about a month. While things had started painfully, I had reached the point where I felt the workouts were helping, and I was even beginning to enjoy them. So I rewarded myself at a Super Bowl party by chowing down on one of my favorite foods: hot wings. I had forgotten how good it felt to eat whatever I wanted and whenever I wanted. On that Sunday night, I felt like a king.

The next morning I walked into the gym and began my usual workout. As I went through the door, I began to feel bad about my feast of hot wings, and I wondered how it would affect my training. I tried to put it out of my mind as I stretched and then got on the treadmill. Things went OK at the beginning, but when I got to the middle of my run, I noticed I was spending a lot more energy than normal. My shirt was soaked with sweat. My heart was racing. The cramp forming in my gut was excruciating, and I started to feel like I was going to have a heart attack. I had been a pretty dedicated workout guy for a month, so I wasn't going to give up. However, things just got worse. Finally, about three quarters of the way through my run, I couldn't take it any more, so I decided to walk for a minute.

I was disgusted at myself and shocked that one day of bad eating affected me so drastically. I was about to vow never to eat hot wings again when I noticed something I will never forget. The grade on the treadmill had been set to two. Normally, the grade is set on zero, or flat, but that day the person before me had decided to walk on an incline and then forgot to put the grade back down. That meant I ran more than two miles *uphill*. It was no wonder that I could feel my heart pounding out of my chest.

Do you ever feel as though God has turned up the grade on the treadmill without you knowing it? We stagger through life out of breath and wonder why God would do something like that to us, especially when it seems like those who aren't trying to serve him are prospering. We wonder why we face persecution, but our search for answers only leaves us asking more questions.

Read Psalm 22

■ Have you ever felt like the psalmist did in this passage?

❑ yes

❑ no

Explain that situation.

_____

_____

_____

_____

_____

_____

■ What kinds of questions about God does suffering cause you to ask?

_____

_____

_____

■ How do you think God feels when you question him in times of suffering?

❏ angry
❏ disappointed
❏ he doesn't care
❏ he invites us to question him

Psalm 22 is a psalm of complaint. A truth that has been passed over for far too long is that God invites us to lift our complaints up to him. For ancient Israel, part of worship was lament, or complaining and crying out to God. In lament, the people of Israel were invited to tell God exactly how they felt. They knew that God already knew their questions and could handle their complaints. Lament was a way the Israelites could express their hearts honestly to God and allow God to meet them where they were.

Too many times we miss the power of lament as we fake our way through worship with God. We hide behind masks, afraid to tell God how we really feel and convinced he would never meet us where we really are. But we all need to know that we don't have to hide anymore. In times of suffering, God invites us to cry out to him and to express our deepest feelings, questions, and emotions. He invites you to complain.

prayer exercise:

Take some time to write out a lament to God. If you are not currently going through a tough time, think back to a time when you were. Use the lament from Jeremiah 20:7-8 printed on the following page as a guide and fill in the blanks to reflect your situation.

"O LORD, you _____ me, and I was _____; you _____ me and prevailed. I am _____ all day long; everyone _____ me. Whenever I speak, I cry out proclaiming _____ and _____. So the word of the LORD has brought me _____ and _____ all day long."

Before you end, read Jeremiah 20:11-13 to see what Jeremiah's lament led him to say. Ask God to bring you to the same truth to which he brought Jeremiah through lament.

when life
falls apart

Read Romans 8:28

Fill in the blanks:

Romans 8:28 says, "And we know that in _____ things God works for the _____ of those who _____ him, who have been _____ according to his purpose."

When I was young, I dreamed of playing college soccer. This dream took me to the soccer field every day after school. Every chance I had, I was out playing soccer with friends or by myself. I loved soccer, and I worked hard to fulfill my dream.

In the fall of 1992, my dream came true. I was a soccer player for a college in Florida. It was one of the greatest years of my life because it was the fulfillment of my lifelong dream. Things were going just as I had hoped until tragedy struck. During my summer break, as I played an indoor game trying to get in shape for my sophomore season, I tore the anterior cruciate ligament (ACL) in my left knee. I was on a breakaway and went to shoot as I had done so many times before. When I did, it felt as though my knee hit the ground. I lied on the floor in pain, not knowing what had happened. I knew I had injured my knee, but I had been hurt before. I spent the next few days hoping my knee would get better. As the swelling went down, I began to walk around, but something was obviously wrong. Every time I planted my left leg, my knee collapsed.

That summer, I was scheduled to go on a tour to coach at soccer camps around the country. Before I left, I went to an orthopedic surgeon to make sure my knee would be OK. As soon as he did the first test on my knee, he knew what had happened. Before the end of that visit to the doctor's office, I knew that I had torn my ACL, that I needed reconstructive surgery, that my summer tour was off and that my sophomore season was over. I had not expected such bad news. It caught me so off guard that I cried on the way home that day, and I am not a person who cries often.

After six months of strenuous rehab, my knee was back to full strength. That spring, I was a leader on my team in offseason workouts, and I was named co-captain for my junior year. I spent the summer doing the camps I had missed the year before. The year of rehab had been hard, but I had overcome. Then, on my first day of fall practice, it happened again. I went to knock the ball away from another player, and my foot got caught in the grass. I tore my left ACL for the second time. I was so frustrated that I tried to play that year with the injury, but by the end of the year it was clear I needed a second surgery. When I woke up after that surgery, my parents told me that the doctors had recommended I end my soccer career.

I don't know if I will ever forget the emotions of that day. It may not seem like a big deal to you, but it was my dream. I wondered, "Why me?" Was God picking on me? I had tried to serve Him my entire life, and this was the thanks I got. I was frustrated, upset, and angry. God had let me down. I spent the next six months trying to figure out how God could allow something like that to happen, but it was no use.

Then one day, my pastor spoke on Romans 8:28. He made a statement that has made all the difference in my life. He said, "Notice the verse does not say that all things are good. Some things are bad. But what God has promised is that he will take even the bad things of our life and work them for good, if we are his children."

Suffering comes in many different ways. Sometimes, our sinful actions cause us to suffer. Sometimes people who are opposed to God inflict suffering on us. And sometimes, suffering comes as an uninvited guest even to those who have followed God their whole lives. I can't tell you how many times I've seen people get their lives right with God only to see their lives fall apart around them. But today, I want you to know that God has done for me what he promises in Romans 8:28. God can take our suffering and use it for our good.

■ Take some time to journal through your story with God today. Use the following questions to guide you.

Describe an event that occurred in your life that you would classify as bad.

_____

_____

_____

_____

How does the promise of Romans 8:28 help you endure the suffering this particular bad tiding may have brought?

_____

_____

_____

_____

How have bad tidings like the one you mentioned worked for your good?

_____

_____

_____

_____

_____

Rest in the peace that God will do
what he has promised in Romans 8:28
in your life. While suffering may
come for a season, the promise of
God is that your suffering is not
in vain. Ask the Holy Spirit to
show you how the promise of this
verse is at work in your life. Rest
in this promise today.

w●rse than
suffering

There is nothing like being on a team. I love the feeling of being connected to others and working alongside them. It's a rewarding experience no matter what kind of team it is. I've played on basketball, football, and golf teams, served on summer camp staff teams and mission trip teams and worked as a part of staff teams. All these teams had one thing in common: everyone worked together to accomplish a common goal. I love being part of a team because it reminds me that I have a purpose to give myself to.

I can't imagine what my life would be like if I had never been part of a team. I'm pretty sure I would be miserable in my job if I weren't walking through life with my co-workers trying to accomplish the same goal. Being surrounded by a group of people who are all seeking to spread the good news of Jesus Christ gives me something to live for. It is hard to fathom life being any other way.

■ Have you been on a team where you felt connected to other people because you had a common goal?

❑ yes
❑ no

What made those experiences memorable?

_____

_____

_____

_____

_____

_____

The book of Acts is a dramatic account of what can happen in the lives of believers when they take the gospel seriously. In Acts 4, Peter and John were imprisoned for what they preached. As we recall from the Gospels, Peter and John had encounters with Christ that forever changed their lives. After they were thrown in prison, the authorities commanded them not to speak or teach about Jesus anymore. But in verse 20, they said, "We cannot help speaking about what we have seen and heard."

Peter and John suffered for the name of Jesus. Church history tells us both eventually lost their lives for the cause of Christ. They did not have the riches of many other people during their time on earth. But they had something even better: Jesus. Because Peter and John had encountered Jesus, they knew that suffering wasn't the worst thing that could happen to them. It would have been far worse for them not to have anything worth suffering for.

Just as I can't imagine life without being a part of a team dedicating itself to the cause of Christ, I can't imagine not having something worth suffering for. Some purposes are so big they are worth the pain. Athletes, students, and entertainers understand this reality and work hard to accomplish their goals. While it's normal for us to try to avoid things that bring pain, to follow God, we must open ourselves to the possibility of suffering. Let's not forget the suffering our Savior Jesus experienced throughout his time on earth. He suffered, so we can't expect to avoid suffering all the time.

God promises he will never leave us during our times of suffering. He is right there beside us, and in the midst of our suffering, we experience his peace and joy. In the end, following God is worth any suffering we may experience. And a life of following God, even with suffering, is far richer than a life that has nothing worth suffering for.

■ What are you living for right now?

_____

_____

_____

_____

■ Do you have a goal in life right now that is worth suffering for?

❑ yes

❑ no

If so, what is it?

_____

_____

_____

prayer exercise:

Are you a person who runs from suffering? Are you taking the gospel seriously enough? Do you count it a joy to have something worth suffering for? As a child of God, these times will come. Every Christian goes through them. Ask God to give you the courage to face these times like Peter and John did. Praise him through your times of suffering. Thank him for giving you something worth suffering for.

Jeremiah
40:1-6

A few weeks ago, my wife and I entered a new phase of our lives when we welcomed our first child, Emma, into the world. To put it mildly, our lives will never be the same. Emma has brought such joy, happiness, laughter and peace to our lives that we often wonder how we ever lived without her. There have been adjustments, and there have been struggles, but through it all it's clear that God had it right when he gave men and women the opportunity to marry and raise a family.

The other day, I was in my office working on this book when God used Emma to give me a picture of himself. My wife dropped by the office to take care of a few things and was heading out to run a few errands. She asked me to watch Emma for a little while. For a couple of minutes, I had the opportunity to hold my daughter. Usually, I don't get that chance until I go home, so I welcomed this escape from the work on my desk.

Emma was a little restless in her car seat, so I picked her up to comfort her in the middle of her distress. As I did so, God clued my ear in to the worship music playing in the background. The moment I picked Emma up, the phrase, "Suddenly I feel you holding me," came up in the song. In that moment, I sensed God showing me himself as I held my daughter.

We began this week by looking at the prophet Jeremiah. We talked about how we can be honest with God, how God works for our good even through our suffering and how having nothing worth suffering for is worse than suffering itself. As we complete our study of the fear of suffering, we come to the truth about God that showed Jeremiah love in the midst of his suffering. It is a promise God made at the beginning of Jeremiah's journey and demonstrated to Jeremiah throughout that journey.

Fill in the blanks:

Jeremiah 1:8 says, "Do not be _____ of them, for I am _____ you and will _____ you, declares the LORD."

Read Jeremiah 40:1-6

■ How did God demonstrate the promise of Jeremiah 1:8 in this passage?

_____

_____

_____

_____

■ Was Jeremiah delivered from every situation?

❑ yes
❑ no

Explain your answer.

_____

_____

_____

_____

■ What truth about God's love does this passage demonstrate?

❑ God is in control of every situation and always has the last word.
❑ God does not desert his followers even though it may feel like he does at times.

❏ God holds onto his children and shepherds them throughout their lives, knowing when to deliver them and when not to.

❏ All of the above

In the end, God used Jeremiah in a powerful way. We benefit from reading the words of this weeping prophet because he trusted God enough to risk suffering. Suffering will come in our lives, even if we make choices designed to help us avoid it. While suffering is never easy, we can take comfort with Jeremiah in the truth that when suffering comes, God himself holds onto us and guides us through. He knows just how much we can bear. He promises never to allow more to happen in our lives than he and we can handle together. In the end, we find that he alone has the last word about suffering in our lives. Today we invite you to experience the love of our Great Shepherd.

prayer exercise:

Take some time to get alone in your room and experience God's love. Play your favorite worship music and listen for God's word for you. As you listen to the songs, reflect on this thought from C.S. Lewis, "God whispers to us in our pleasures, speaks in our conscience, but shouts in our pains: it is his megaphone to rouse a deaf world." (C. S. Lewis, *The Problem of Pain*, [New York: Collier Books, 1962], 93.)

_____

_____

_____

_____

_____

_____

_____

_____

_____

_____

_____

This page is designed to give you space to take notes during your "Dismantled" group session or to journal your reflections on the highlights of this week's study.

DISMANTLED

FEAR OF REJECTION

moses (part 1):
struggling
toward trust

face to face
with rejection

Have you ever walked into a room and thought someone was waving you over to sit with them, only to find out, as you got closer, that person was really waving at someone else? If you are like me, you know just how rejection situations like that can make you feel. You thought you knew the person. It was great to see someone excited that you had walked into the room. But just as quickly as acceptance catapulted you out of an otherwise ho-hum day, rejection sent you spiraling.

Rejection is a hard pill for us to swallow. It's not something anyone hopes for. When it comes our way, it has the potential to destroy our self-confidence or at least introduce doubt about how valuable we really are. Many of us fear rejection so much that we avoid it at all costs. We will do anything to be accepted. And if being accepted is not an option, we would rather be unknown than known and unwanted.

This week we are coming face to face with the fear of rejection in our lives. This subtle yet powerful foe has influenced and paralyzed thousands of individuals. Rejection holds many of us captive and keeps us from realizing God's best for our lives. Moses' story demonstrates the power of the fear of rejection and shows how God longs to love us through it.

Read Exodus 2:1-15

■ How does Moses encounter acceptance in this passage?

_____

_____

_____

_____

■ How does Moses encounter rejection in this passage?

_____

_____

_____

_____

_____

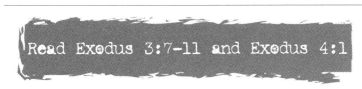

Read Exodus 3:7-11 and Exodus 4:1

■ How did the fear of rejection affect Moses later in his life?

❏ He didn't want to do what God called him to do.

❏ It had no affect on him at all.

❏ It equipped him to accomplish the task God called him to do.

Moses got his first taste of rejection early in life. He had grown up under the acceptance of Pharaoh's court. But his first action recorded in Exodus got him thrown out of the country and sent him running for his life. As in the opening illustration, Moses experienced temporary acceptance that quickly turned the other way. By the time we get to Exodus 3-4, it's no wonder Moses had so many reservations about following God's call to go back to Egypt.

■ Has the fear of rejection ever made you not want to do something you felt God was calling you to do?

❏ yes

❏ no

If so, explain that situation.

_____

_____

_____

_____

_____

■ How often do you fear rejection?

❑ every day
❑ once a week
❑ once a month
❑ once a year
❑ once in a lifetime
❑ never

If we are honest, most of us, like Moses, will admit that we would rather avoid rejection than face it. But God in his love was not content for Moses to be paralyzed by the fear of rejection. This week, we will see how God wants to love us through the fear of rejection in our lives as well.

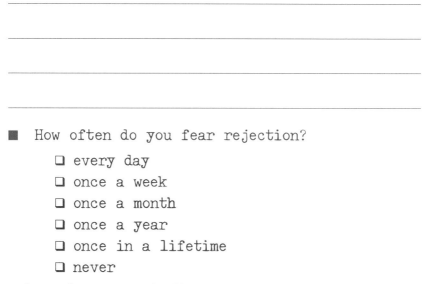

prayer exercise:

Ask God to help you have the courage to face the fear of rejection this week. Take a moment to write out a prayer telling God why this fear has so much control in our lives. In this prayer, ask God to help you through the emotions, scars and hurt that you have experienced, and ask him to help you embrace his calling on your life.

our need
to be known and loved

1 John
4:7-10

■ Do you think it is selfish to want to be
   loved by God and other people?

   ❑ yes
   ❑ no

Why or why not?

_____

_____

_____

_____

We all want to be known and loved, whether we admit it or not. This
need is a powerful force that we will do almost anything to fill. We will even
settle for acceptance from peers, doing whatever we have to do to gain it,
instead of being truly known and loved. So many people go through life as
double agents, acting one way in one place and completely differently in
another so they can be accepted wherever they are, instead of living with
integrity and being accepted for who they really are.

Our desire to be known and loved is not bad. God created us with this
need. The problem comes when we try to earn acceptance and love from
others, because only God can truly meet this need. When we live under the
reality of God's love and acceptance, we can truly be ourselves. If others
accept us for who we are, that's great. If not, we can rest in the fact that
God himself loves us.

■ Which statement is true?

   ❑ I'm loved because I'm valuable.
   ❑ I'm valuable because I'm loved by God.

I love the pecan pie my wife's grandmother makes. It's the most delicious food I have ever put in my mouth. I get excited every time we go to my wife's hometown in Georgia because I know that I'll get to have some of Mimi's pecan pie. Once when we were there, I saw a huge bucket of pecans sitting in the corner. I walked over, picked a few up and started looking at them. I felt as though I needed to thank them for the hundreds of pieces of pecan pie I had enjoyed over the years. But a thought hit me as I looked at the pecans. Not once in all of the times I had eaten Mimi's pie did I think about where the pecans came from. I never considered where this delicious food came from. I know it's not profound, but pecans come from pecan trees. Now, whenever I enjoy pecan pie, I think about how thankful I am for pecan trees.

Just as pecan trees are the true source of pecan pie, God is the true source of love. Too many of us live as if something we do leads to love. But our value comes from the fact that God freely loves us.

Read 1 John 4:7-10

Fill in the blanks:
First John 4:7a says, "Dear friends, let us _____ one another, for _____ comes from God."

This passage in 1 John gives us an amazing description of where love comes from. Perhaps the greatest definition of God is this: God is love. God does not intend for the Christian life to be lived alone. God intends for us to live within a loving community. We usually find the most joy in our walks with God as we journey through life with a group of people and experience true love and acceptance. Think about it: God himself lives in community through the trinity: God the Father, God the Son and God the Holy Spirit. Our need to be known and loved is legitimate. Let us accept the fact that God wants us to experience the joy of being known and loved.

■ What are some things in your life that have made you feel rejected?

_____

_____

■ If someone rejects us, does it mean God also rejects us?

  ❑ yes
  ❑ no

Explain your answer.

_____

_____

_____

_____

We are accepted by God through the sacrifice of his son. When you give your life to Jesus Christ, you don't have to fear rejection from the Father anymore. We are completely acceptable in God's sight because of what Jesus did for us. We can approach the Father with boldness through the blood of Jesus Christ and enjoy his acceptance. This is how we can face the fear of rejection in our lives. The next time you feel rejected and feel the need to be loved and known, remember this: love comes from God. He invented it. And when you enjoy the feeling of being loved and accepted, don't forget where it comes from. Just as I thank the pecan trees for pecans, thank God for love.

prayer exercise:

Spend this time thanking the Father for being the inventor of acceptance and love. Ask him to show you how to be a person full of love for him and for others. Spend a few moments in silence enjoying the acceptance you have in God. Smile and remember that God wants you to experience his acceptance.

the reality
of rejection

When I was in tenth grade, my one big desire was to make the junior-varsity basketball team. I never worried about it, because I had been an all-conference player for my ninth-grade team. That was one of my greatest sports accomplishments. I was so confident I would make the team that I wondered why I needed to try out. But the morning the team was posted, I looked for my name, and it wasn't there. I thought there must have been a mistake. I couldn't believe I didn't make the team. It was one of the most embarrassing moments of my life. A week later, the girl I had been dating for more than two years broke up with me. I thought my life was coming apart. The reality of rejection hit so close to home that it overwhelmed me. I wondered if I was good enough for anyone. I felt alone and worthless. It took me more than a year to get over those two rejections. The reality of rejection is intense. Even now, when I think back on that time in my life, I shake my head remembering how much pain I went through.

■ Why do you think rejection hurts so much?

_____

_____

_____

_____

_____

_____

_____

■ How do you think you would have felt if you were in Joseph's shoes?

_____

_____

_____

_____

_____

_____

Joseph knew all about rejection. His brothers were so jealous of him that they threw him into a pit and then sold him into slavery. That wasn't the end of rejection for Joseph. He was falsely accused of rape. He was thrown in prison and forgotten. He was probably tempted to believe God had rejected him too. But that was not the case. God stepped into the middle of Joseph's rejection and made sense of it all. God does this to our fears as well. He steps into the middle of them and has something to say.

We learned yesterday that we are accepted by God. But this doesn't mean rejection is easy. Rejection is real, and it is painful. No one in his right mind wants to be rejected. Most of us will still experience rejection. In the midst of our fear of rejection, we have to hang onto the truth that rejection by others does not mean we are worthless. People are always going to let us down. The best thing we can do in moments of rejection is place our focus on God. He does not reject his children. He accepts and loves us. There would be no rejection worse than being rejected by God. But we don't need to fear that. He showed how much he longs to accept and love us by sending his son to die for us. If you are a Christian, you can celebrate the fact that you don't need to fear rejection. People will let us down, but our Father will not.

Say the following prayer out loud:

Lord, I give you my life, and
I submit to your authority.
Father, sometimes life is so
hard and painful. You know the
times that I have been
rejected. I ask that you take
this pain and burden from me.
I don't want to carry it
anymore. I thank you that you
have something to say about
this. Lord, just as you
stepped into Joseph's
situation, please step into
mine. I give this fear to you
and trust you to take care of
me. I love you, and I pray in
the strong name of Jesus
Christ, Amen.

Now, use the space below to write a letter to
yourself. Write out the truths that God speaks
into your fear of rejection. Write about how
God accepts and loves you. This will be a
great reminder of the truth about how God
feels about you.

DISMANTLED: FEAR OF REJECTION

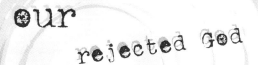

our rejected God

Isaiah 53:3

I will never forget the day I learned to drive a stick shift. My buddy Richard rode shotgun as I took his car onto the neighborhood streets. I about gave us both whiplash as I jerked the car all over the road. The problem wasn't that I failed to listen to Richard. The problem was that what he said didn't resonate with me. So, I was trying to learn by doing my own thing. I wanted to do it my way, not the right way. After about thirty minutes, Richard got pretty mad and told me to pull over and get out. I convinced him I would start listening and do what he said. Sure enough, his way worked, and I learned how to drive the car.

■ Do you ever wander away from Jesus and try to live your life your own way?

☐ yes
☐ no

Read Isaiah 53:3

Fill in the blanks:

Isaiah 53:3 says, "He was _____ and _____ by men, a man of _____, and familiar with _____. Like one from whom men hide their faces he was _____, and we esteemed him not."

■ What did Jesus know about rejection?

_____

_____

_____

_____

■ How did Jesus experience rejection? List as many examples as you can think of.

_____

_____

_____

_____

■ How do you think rejection affected Jesus?

❑ He ignored it.

❑ He fought back.

❑ He did whatever he had to do to be accepted.

❑ He gave up on his mission.

❑ He relied on the acceptance of God instead of the acceptance of men.

This verse is a very uncomfortable one. We like to think of happy and pleasant pictures of Jesus. We don't enjoy meditating on scriptures that show us the real and unpleasant pain he experienced. He was beaten, made fun of, spit on, run out of town and eventually executed as a common criminal. Jesus experienced rejection, and he told us that we could expect to experience it as well.

Too often, when we face the threat of rejection, we run our own way, convinced God doesn't know what he is doing. In this verse, we see that it doesn't have to be that way. Our God faced rejection, and we can too. This means that, when rejection comes our way, we can trust Jesus to be there in the midst of it. He understands the rejection we experience. Instead of running from rejection, we need to be willing to suffer as Christ did. He will not leave us when others reject us. As a matter of fact, times of rejection may be some of the greatest spiritual markers in our lives.

■ How can Jesus meet us in the midst of our
rejection?

_____

_____

_____

_____

prayer exercise:

Do you have a tendency to do your
own thing too often? Do you look
for ways to avoid the very pains
our Savior suffered? Do you run
from your fears instead of facing
them? If so, you are not alone.
Confess to the Lord that you need
him to help you in these areas. Ask
him to forgive you for trying to do
things your own way instead of
listening to him and obeying what
he wants in your life. Tell him you
will embrace rejection if that is
what he wants you to do. Make him
master of your life today.

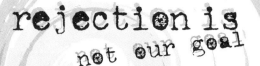

Acts
17: 16-34

When I was in high school, my church youth group had a weekend ski retreat in West Virginia. We had a great time skiing and worshiping together. The speaker that weekend was very energetic and challenged everyone to take a stand for Christ. But although I'm sure the speaker meant well, his message didn't get through. I came out of that weekend thinking that Christians were supposed to pursue rejection and that, if we weren't being rejected, we weren't truly living the Christian life. As a teenager, I carried around a lot of guilt because I wasn't being rejected by my peers.

Things were quite the opposite for me. The Christian friends in my group were influencers, and people, including non-Christians, loved hanging around us. I carried around so much false guilt during those years. I wish someone had told me that the goal of the Christian life is not to pursue rejection but to pursue Christ. Most Christians will at some point be rejected for what they believe, but rejection is not our goal. Whether we face a little rejection or a lot, if rejection comes, it comes. We must pursue Christ instead of feeling an obligation or self-righteousness about being rejected for our faith.

■ Have you ever been led to believe that, if you're not being rejected, you're not truly following Christ?

❏ yes
❏ no

If so, explain that situation.

_____

_____

_____

_____

■ What would it look like if you were so determined to face rejection for what you believe that you missed Christ in the process?

_____

_____

_____

■ Why do you think some people are drawn to this mindset?

_____

_____

_____

Read Acts 17:16-34

This passage gives us a great example of how believers should act around people who don't have relationships with Christ. On a missionary journey, Paul stopped in Athens, Greece. During this time, Athens was a place where many religions and philosophies came together. People who lived there worshiped many different gods. When Paul arrived in Athens, he walked around and observed the different statues and idols. Notice what Paul did not do. He did not start screaming in the town center and stirring up trouble. He was not pursuing rejection. If Paul had wanted to be rejected, he could have gone into Athens like a bully looking for a fight.

But that's not what Paul did. When he got the chance to speak, he made mention of an altar to an unknown God and began his message there. God used Paul that day, and it is important for us to realize how Paul related the good news of the gospel. He pursued Jesus, not rejection. We know that Paul was rejected many times throughout his life, and we should expect rejection to come our way at times as well. But while God calls us to experience rejection at times, he does not call us to seek it out.

■ Does choosing not to pursue rejection mean that we will never experience it?

❏ yes

❏ no

■ What is the difference between pursuing rejection and expecting it?

_____

_____

_____

_____

_____

_____

We need to realize that we do not have to stand on street corners and scream the name of Jesus to follow God. Our witness does not have to be obnoxious and rude. We can be relational and allow other people to see Jesus in us in the way we talk and the way we live our lives. We can expect to experience rejection at times as we follow God. We can hold onto the promises of God we have learned this week during those moments. The point of the Christian journey is not to pursue rejection by men but to be accepted by God. God wants us to enjoy him and his presence.

Ask the Father to teach you how to let the world see the light inside you. Tell him that you don't want to run away from rejection but that you don't want rejection to be your goal either. Tell God you want to pursue him. Ask him to teach you how to follow his ways.

_____

_____

_____

_____

_____

_____

_____

_____

_____

_____

_____

_____

_____

This page is designed to give you space to take notes during your "Dismantled" group session or to journal your reflections on the highlights of this week's study.

DISMANTLED

FEAR OF FAILURE

moses (part 2):
connecting with a
God who never fails

face to face
with failure

Have you ever noticed the way two people can look at the same thing but see it completely differently? Probably one of the greatest examples of this is the way guys and girls see food. Girls are looking for atmosphere. They want to eat at places where food is presented beautifully. They would rather the food be color-coordinated than be filling. They want sandwiches you can daintily eat with your fingertips. Guys are just the opposite. Guys want to get bloated. They don't care what food looks like as long as it tastes good and there is enough of it. They don't want sandwiches you eat with your fingertips. They want sandwiches that barely fit in your mouth, sandwiches so full they have a good chance of spilling all over your shirt.

Chad and I had a first-hand experience of this difference when we invited our wives to join us for lunch at a restaurant we discovered close to our office. Actually, it isn't a restaurant; it's a grill located in a gas station convenience store. (Guys are able to find a four-course meal at the gas station.) Our wives were not amused with our discovery. We knew we were in trouble when Chad's wife called from the pay phone *just outside* the gas station to say she couldn't find the restaurant anywhere. Needless to say, while we still eat at Riding's Quick Shop on occasion, our wives have never been back.

Just as guys and girls see food differently, we look at failure much differently than God does. We get so wrapped up in the things we do that we often equate ourselves with those things. When we fail at something, we think we are failures. But God sees things differently. He sees us for who we are, not what we do. He sees failure not as something that defines us but as a learning experience he can use to continue to make us into the people he wants us to be. Last week, we looked at the fear of rejection through the life of Moses. This week, we continue looking at Moses' journey to examine the fear of failure, a fear that often accompanies the fear of rejection.

■ What was Moses' response when God called him to bring his message?

  ❏ He accepted God's call.

  ❏ He tried to excuse himself from God's call because he felt inadequate.

■ How did the fear of failure affect Moses in these passages?

_____

_____

_____

_____

■ Have you ever felt God calling you to do something you thought would lead to failure?

    ❏ yes

    ❏ no

If so, how did you handle that situation?

_____

_____

_____

_____

Moses' fear of failure became a power that hindered him from following God. Probably because he was tormented by past failures, as we talked about last week, Moses was afraid to do what God had called him to do. The same often happens to us.

Moses wrestled with the same questions about failure that we do. What does it mean to be successful? What is failure? These are questions worth asking as we begin this week. Sometimes we have a tendency to see success and failure as opposites, and to some extent they are very different. But we sometimes think that being successful means never failing, and that's just not true. It took Thomas Edison many attempts to invent the light bulb. It took Michael Jordan years to win an NBA championship. Dan Marino never won a Super Bowl. But none of us would consider these people failures. They are our heroes, people we call successes, yet each of them experienced failure. And there are many more like them.

The same is true in our spiritual lives. Living life successfully is not the same as never making a mistake. We will make mistakes. After all, we are human. Jesus, God in the flesh, was the only person who never made a mistake. But despite our mistakes, we can be successful, because success is determined by how we recover from our mistakes. Michael Irvin, after losing a playoff game, said, "Failure is the greatest motivator." The next year his Dallas Cowboys team won the Super Bowl. Living successful Christian lives is about recovering from mistakes, taking God at his word, and living for him.

prayer exercise:

Take some time to list some of your past failures. If you don't have any failures, you may not have ever tried anything, or at least anything God-sized. Take some time to reflect on how these failures either hold you back or push you forward. Ask God to take the failures that hold you back and teach you from them. Allow the Holy Spirit to guide you as you learn to learn from failure.

the root
of the fear of failure

People love gumballs. If you don't believe it, look around the next time you go to a restaurant or a grocery store. Chances are that there will be a gumball machine there, and you probably won't have to watch long to see someone buy one. It's like those machines have a hypnotic power that draws people to them and forces them to pop in a quarter. We know we're paying twenty-five cents for a three-cent gumball, but the five-minute sugar rush that comes when we put these spheres in our mouths is worth it.

Gumballs come in all shapes and sizes. One idea taking malls by storm is the Gumball Gourmet. When I first saw it, I stood in awe, as if I had discovered a whole new world. In one booth, the Gumball Gourmet has 40 machines with 40 different flavors of gumballs: blueberry pie, peach cobbler, cotton candy, caramel popcorn and just about any flavor you can imagine. People from all over the mall come to get their favorite kind. And one taste of each exotic flavor makes you think that the gumball world just doesn't get any better than the Gumball Gourmet.

Every once in a while, we come across something that challenges our view of things. It is no different with gumballs. As a gumball lover, I loved trying the different flavors at the Gumball Gourmet whenever I shopped at the mall with my wife. But one day at the mall I saw something I had never seen before, and it changed my life. It was the Mega-Mouth Gumball machine. This life-changing piece of gum is huge—a full three inches in diameter. It makes a thud, not a tink, when it comes out of the machine. It's more than just a post-dinner snack; it's a meal in itself.

I was overwhelmed when I saw it, and I just had to have one. So, I bummed two quarters off of my wife and bought one. I took it to my friend's house—he's a fellow gumball lover—to show him what I'd found. I tried to get the whole thing in my mouth, but I couldn't. And the sugar rush I got from eating that thing was enough to keep an elephant up all night. I thought I knew what gumballs were, but then I encountered the Mega-Mouth Gumball, and now I see the world of gumballs completely differently.

Many times we think small thoughts of God. We know some of the different flavors of his character, such as grace, holiness, and love. But we don't understand just how mega-sized God is. This leads to big problems, as Nebuchadnezzar learned.

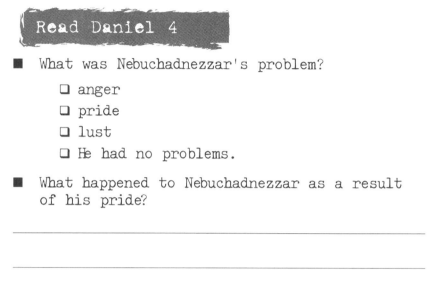

Read Daniel 4

■ What was Nebuchadnezzar's problem?
- ❏ anger
- ❏ pride
- ❏ lust
- ❏ He had no problems.

■ What happened to Nebuchadnezzar as a result of his pride?

_____

_____

_____

_____

Nebuchadnezzar was the king of the greatest empire of his day. He was the most powerful man in the world, and his success went to his head. He began to get an inflated view of himself and a deflated view of God. In fact, he began to equate himself with God. But one day, Nebuchadnezzar came into contact with God. In that moment, as a madman grazing in the field, he saw how big God was and how small he was. All his previous views about himself were challenged, and Nebuchadnezzar saw how dependent upon God he really was.

Nebuchadnezzar suffered from pride as a result of his success, but pride is also at the root of the fear of failure. Those of us who fear failure are usually afraid of being seen as weak or not good at something. We are afraid that our smallness will be exposed. We are afraid that if people see our smallness, they will reject us. So we hide, hoping that people will only see the big things we do well. This explains why so many people who are tremendously successful suffer from the fear of failure the most.

We suffer from the same problem Nebuchadnezzar did. Many times, we have an inflated view of ourselves and a deflated view of God. This pride leads us to fear failure in unhealthy ways. The answer for us, just as it was for Nebuchadnezzar, is to see God for who he really is. We need to get a picture of our Mega-Mouth-sized God.

prayer exercise:

Take a prayer walk outside today. Notice throughout God's creation how big God is. As you walk around in an attitude of prayer, ask God to help you get a God-sized picture of him. Ask him to fill your life with that truth so that, when you face the fear of failure, you stop looking at yourself and start looking at God.

DISMANTLED: FEAR OF FAILURE

God's response
to man's failure

Genesis 12:1-3

The first 11 chapters of Genesis tell of the growing evil actions of man. The book of Genesis begins with the story of how God created the heavens and the earth. Creation reached its climax as God created man and woman in his own image. God placed Adam and Eve in the Garden of Eden and gave them authority over the animals. Everything was at their disposal. There was only one thing they were not to do: eat from the tree of the knowledge of good and evil. Adam and Eve knew no sin and had God's blessing and presence upon them as they lived in the garden. But by the end of Genesis 3, Adam and Eve had done the one thing they were told not to do. They sinned, and as a consequence of sin they later died. The next eight chapters of Genesis tell about men and women in their fallen condition. In Genesis 6, God wiped out much of creation with a worldwide flood because of the evil people did. In Genesis 11, people sought to bring glory to themselves by building a tower at Babel to reach God. God did not allow this, confusing the language of the people and causing them to scatter over the face of the earth.

Read Genesis 12:1-3

■ What was God's answer to man's failure?
- ❏ He ignored man.
- ❏ He left man to find out an answer for himself.
- ❏ He used Abram to begin his greatest work, the work of restoration.

The great news of Genesis 12:1-3 is that, in the midst of a world of incredible sinfulness, God acted. He called one man to bless all the nations of the world. Through Abram, the nation of Israel was established. And from this nation, God would send his Son Jesus as a sacrifice to redeem and restore people who believed in him.

Fill in the blanks:

Genesis 12:3b says, "And _____ _____ on _____ will be _____ through you."

God came to Abram and told him to "go to the land I will show you." This passage is the hinge of the entire Old Testament. As Abram obeyed, God promised to make Abram into a great nation, to bless him and to make his name great. God promised to bless those who blessed Abram and curse those who cursed Abram and said all the peoples of the earth would be blessed through him. The great news of the rest of the Bible is that God did what he said he would do. As Christians, we understand Jesus as the ultimate fulfillment of this promise. What did God do when mankind failed? He worked.

■ If God produced restoration and redemption from the greatest failure of all of time, how can he work in spite of your failure?

_____

_____

_____

_____

The good news of the gospel is God's answer to man's failure. If God can produce the gospel from sin, think what he is capable of doing in spite of our failures. Failure is not the end for God. He specializes in taking failure and redeeming it. He is a master at restoration. He creates beauty from ashes.

Think back to the ways God has worked in your life. Think about the times you have failed and the ways God redeemed and restored that failure. These failures may be moral failures, or simply a time when you tried something and it didn't work.

- How has God used these failures in your life?

_____

_____

_____

_____

- Now, in an exercise of creativity, draw two pictures that demonstrate how God has redeemed failure in your life. These pictures don't have to be great works of art; they are meant to help you reflect on and demonstrate how God has worked in your life.

prayer exercise:

Using the pictures you have drawn, meditate on the work of God in your life. Thank God for being a God who can take failure and work it for good in your life.

DISMANTLED: FEAR OF FAILURE

the God who never fails

Deuteronomy
30: 11-20

Now that we are well into the 21st Century, it is hard to believe how much anxiety the year 2000 produced across the world. Many people doubted whether we would make it into the new millennium. December 31, 1999, was a day of great anxiety and fear. No one knew what would happen when our computers rolled over to the year 2000. The world spent millions and millions of dollars fixing computer glitches before Y2K, hoping to avoid a major shutdown. And for the most part, it worked.

I remember watching the festivities around the world that day, anxiously waiting to see what would happen as we entered the year 2000. I have to admit that, even though I'm an optimist, I had my questions too. I wondered if the world would go spinning out of control. I wondered if God would show up in a display of power to call the whole world to his glory. I watched throughout the day as Hong Kong, Paris, London, New York, Chicago and Los Angeles celebrated. The stunning fireworks shows at the Eiffel Tower and in England, New York, and Washington, D.C., were marvelous. I wondered as I watched if God was at least a little impressed with our festivities.

At one point that day, I watched the sun come up over New Zealand for the first time in the 21st century. It was a marvelous sunrise, but it was pretty much the same sunrise that happens nearly every day. And I might not have even noticed it except for the fact that I had so eagerly anticipated God's action that day. As I watched that sunrise, I saw a work of God I miss out on most days. The sun rose, displayed its majesty and set that night. It was not bothered by Y2K either. And the truth is it was never in any danger. The sun didn't need to be fixed. It will rise as long as God wants it to.

I learned a lesson in front of my television set that day. Nothing can thwart God's work. While things may seem bleak at times, and sometimes it seems as though the prince of darkness rules over this world, God is in control. He has yet to make a mistake. He has never frantically rushed around trying to correct a glitch and keep his systems from shutting down. God confidently sees his plan through to the very last moment. He's way ahead of the game.

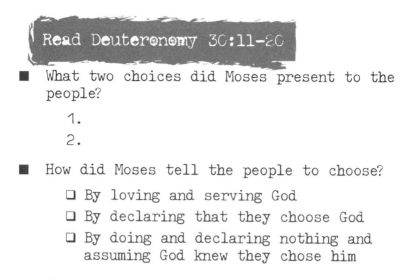

■ What two choices did Moses present to the people?

    1.

    2.

■ How did Moses tell the people to choose?

    ❑ By loving and serving God

    ❑ By declaring that they choose God

    ❑ By doing and declaring nothing and assuming God knew they chose him

In this passage, we see Moses at the end of his last pep talk to the nation of Israel. Summing up his entire ministry, he asked the Israelites to decide what side to spend their lives on. They could choose God's side, which Moses said would ultimately lead to life and prosperity. Or they could choose the other side, which Moses said would surely lead to death and destruction. He challenged the people to hold fast to God, because he is the God who never fails. When God wants to do something, he does it. Moses reminded the people that if they rallied to God's side, obeyed his commandments, and followed him, God would direct their path.

There is great confidence in serving the Lord because God determines what success really is. If we are on his side, we will ultimately be successful. Sure, there will be times when we don't succeed by the world's standards. We may not own the biggest houses, make the most money, or have the most fame or power. But the truth is, at the end of the story, we are successful because our God holds success in his hand. As someone once said, "I've read the end of the book, and we win." We need not fear failure, because we do not determine our own success. We can be successful because God holds success in his hand.

Use the following questions to help you reflect on the truth about your life.

■ Weigh your activities today in light of eternity. What activities are you investing in that show that you have rallied to God's side?

_____

_____

_____

■ What activities are you investing in because you are seeking success by the world's standards? (These do not necessarily have to be bad things.)

_____

_____

_____

■ Which set of activities most defines you?
   ❏ those on God's side
   ❏ those on the world's side

■ How can you organize your life to make God's activities a priority instead of the world's activities?

_____

_____

_____

_____

Ask God to make his desires the desires of your heart. As you seek to better organize your activities, ask God to reveal to you how you can organize your life to get on God's side.

what do you want
on your epitaph?

Deuteronomy
34:1-12

Marketing is the art of creating a perceived need and then advertising a product to meet that need. If it is done well, people will buy even the most outrageous things. One of the greatest illustrations of this is the pet rock fad that swept across the country in 1975.

Gary Dahl was hanging out with some friends one night when the conversation turned to pets. His friends talked about their pets, and Gary complained about how much trouble dogs, cats, and fish were. He told his friends he had a pet that made no mess, cost next to nothing, and had a carefree personality. It was a pet rock. The group started talking about the possibilities of marketing a pet rock, and a few weeks later, a phenomenon was born.

In August, Dahl introduced the Pet Rock gift box, which included the *Pet Rock Training Manual* and a Rosarita Beach stone (a gray pebble that sold for a penny), at a gift show in San Francisco. By Christmas, *Newsweek* had run an article on the invention, Gary had appeared on *The Tonight Show with Johnny Carson* twice and more than half of the newspapers in the country had run stories on pet rocks. In a few months, more than a million Pet Rock packages sold for $3.95 each.

Think about that for a second. More than a million people were convinced to spend $3.95 on a rock, and they actually thought they bought a pet. While I'm not old enough to remember the start of the pet rock craze, I do remember some of my friends buying them. I remember even being a little jealous of my friend's pet rock. But now I realize it was just a rock.

Today, there are no pet rocks. People eventually woke up to the reality that they had bought a rock, not a pet. But we do buy into other hollow promises. We buy workout machines that promise to bulk us up or slim us down in five easy minutes a day. We pay money to name stars after people. (OK, I did that, but it was my wife's birthday, and it seemed like a sweet thing to do.) While companies measure their success by sales numbers, those of us who buy these products question whether the products themselves are really successful.

The same thing is true in our lives spiritually. At some point, we are all tempted to pursue something less than what God has called us to, tempted to measure success by sales numbers instead of the impact we have on people. Moses was tempted to think this way when God called him. But God loved Moses out of that desire and birthed in him a greater desire for what God could do through him.

Read Deuteronomy 34:1-12

Fill in the blanks:

Deuteronomy 34:10-12 says, "Since then, _____ prophet has risen in Israel like _____, whom the LORD knew _____ to _____, who did all those _____ _____ and _____ the LORD sent him to do in _____ to Pharaoh and to all his officials and to his whole land. For _____ _____ has ever shown the _____ _____ or _____ the _____ deeds that _____ did in the sight of all Israel."

President Woodrow Wilson said, "I would rather fail at something that will ultimately succeed than succeed at something that will ultimately fail." That's a great insight that applies to our spiritual lives. The fear of failure often keeps us from pursuing God's best for our lives. Instead of investing our lives in things that really matter, we settle for success in lesser things. Like Gary Dahl with his pet rocks, we are content to measure our success by short-term personal benefits rather than the long-term benefits to God's kingdom. Despite his fear of failure, Moses decided to invest his life in something bigger than himself. Moses never made it to the Promised Land, which would make him look like a failure on the world's scales of success. But his epitaph read, "Here lies the greatest prophet Israel ever knew." God turned a pathetic shepherd who was afraid of failure into Israel's greatest prophet.

■ Write an epitaph that reflects how you hope to be remembered after you die.

_____

_____

_____

_____

_____

_____

■ What needs to happen to ensure that you are remembered this way?

_____

_____

_____

■ How does the fear of failure hold you back from this hope?

_____

_____

_____

_____

_____

■ How does what you've learned from Moses' story give you hope?

_____

_____

_____

_____

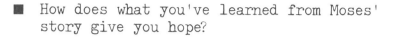

prayer exercise:

Spend some time asking God to make you a part of something bigger than yourself. Then ask him to help you identify what that could be as you look for ways to be involved in your local church. Take time to listen for his answer.

This page is designed to give you space to take notes during your "Dismantled" group session or to journal your reflections on the highlights of this week's study.

DISMANTLED

FEAR OF BEING ALONE

elijah:
the power of
christian community

face to face
with loneliness

Choosing to follow God often opens us up to the possibility of loneliness. This scares us, because the fear of being alone is one of the most powerful forces in our lives. It's not that we're afraid we will choose to be alone. Instead, we're afraid of being left alone. Far too often, the fear of being alone grips our hearts and influences our decisions. It's the reason our peers have so much influence on us, whether for good or for bad. This fear affects how we share Christ, the way we stand for Christ, what we do and how we do it.

■ **Have you ever felt that, if you got serious about God and his things, you would be alone?**

❏ yes
❏ no

Many of us have experienced the reality of this fear. My wife certainly did. Kim faced some pretty tough decisions her junior year of high school. She had been on a mission trip where she experienced God in a way that changed her outlook and what was important to her. But when she returned, the fear of being alone became an all-too-present force in her life. Up to that point, she had all the friends she could want. She was a four-sport athlete and a member of the homecoming court. But her newfound passion for God and his things made her friends uncomfortable. Before she knew it, her friends turned on her, and day after day she experienced the pain of being alone. Her old friends mocked her, spread rumors about her and even went so far as to spray-paint a nasty message about her on a bridge in the middle of her small town. Kim learned that a passion for Christ can lead to ridicule from those who are passionate about other things. She spent many days and nights wondering if the change in her life was worth it.

The prophet Elijah's story is very similar. He is probably one of the most well known prophets in Israel's history, second only to Moses, whom we studied the last two weeks. Elijah witnessed and took part in many God-sized events in his life. But throughout his journey, Elijah was plagued by the thought that he was the only one left serving God, and his fear of being alone gnawed at his heart.

Read 1 Kings 19:1-10

Fill in the blanks:

First Kings 19:10 says, "He replied, 'I have been very _____ for the LORD God Almighty. The _____ have rejected your _____, broken down your _____, and put your _____ to _____ with the sword. I am the _____ one left, and now they are trying to _____ me too.'"

■ How did the fear of being alone make Elijah feel?

❑ motivated
❑ excited
❑ depressed
❑ scared

■ Does it surprise you to see a prophet of God acting this way?

❑ yes
❑ no

Explain your answer.

_____

_____

_____

_____

_____

■ Have you ever felt like Elijah did in this passage?

 ❑ yes
 ❑ no

If yes, briefly describe such an experience.

_____

_____

_____

_____

■ How has the fear of being alone held you back in your walk with God?

_____

_____

_____

_____

Elijah came face to face with the fear of being alone. The same man who called down fire from heaven worried that he was the only person standing for God. Queen Jezebel had made threats on Elijah's life, and he fled to the desert. In this passage, Elijah was isolated, angry, depressed, and lonely.

Like Elijah, we often look for the easy way out. We know that God has done great things in our past, and we want to serve him with our futures, but the present gives us a lot of trouble. We long to let our passion for God out, but we have been burned by it before, so we keep that passion hidden inside. Sometimes, the fear of being alone gnaws at us so much that we decide to follow God a little less passionately. And sometimes when we let our passion for God show, like Elijah, we end up rejected, depressed, and angry, and we question whether following God is worth it.

This week we are going to think about the fear of being alone. We will talk about how sometimes being alone is a good thing. We will look at the creation story to see what God thinks about loneliness. We'll study community and the role it plays in our lives. And then, we will rejoin Elijah, and see how God loved him through the fear of being alone.

prayer exercise:

Ask God to help you identify this fear's ~~roots in your life~~. Spend some time asking God to help you through the fear of being alone. Remember that you can be honest with God about all of your feelings, frustrations, and anxieties. If you are not struggling with this fear at this time, pray for someone you know who is.

when . . .
being alone is good

Matthew
14:13-14

I love being with people. I'm an extrovert, so I get energized when I'm around others. If it were up to me, I'd hang out with friends every night of the week. But a few years ago, I learned a lesson that has changed my lifestyle. At the time, I was frustrated about the lack of intimacy in my walk with God. I just felt stale in my relationship with him. I prayed about this and told the Father that I wanted to be closer to him. A couple of weeks passed, and I was still frustrated about it, so I prayed again. I didn't hear a voice or have a vision, but I felt like God was telling me to look back at my calendar from the past two weeks. When I did, I saw I had done something all day and every night over those two weeks. My schedule was slammed with activities. The things I had done were not bad in themselves. But there was a problem. If I was always busy doing things and always around other people, how could I expect to hear God and enjoy closeness with him? It is not that being with people is bad. But we have to have a break where we can have time being alone before God.

■ How much alone time do you spend during your week?

  ❑ none
  ❑ thirty minutes
  ❑ one hour
  ❑ two or more hours

■ Are you comfortable being alone in silence?

  ❑ yes
  ❑ no

Why or why not?

_____

_____

_____

_____

Read Matthew 14:13-14

Jesus was a busy man. People constantly bombarded him from every angle with all sorts of requests. And Jesus loved being with people, healing them, talking to them, and showing them love. Most of the stories about Jesus in the Gospels show him with people. But every once in a while, we see a glimpse of Jesus retreating to be alone with the Father. This passage is one of those glimpses.

Notice that when Jesus comes back from being by himself, he sees a group of people and has compassion for them. It was in times of solitude that the Father gave his Son the strength to go about his business. Jesus was energized by his time alone. He loved being around people, but he also cherished his quiet time.

■ Why do you think Jesus withdrew from the crowds and spent quiet time with his Father?

_____

_____

_____

_____

_____

■ Why is it important for you to do the same?

_____

_____

_____

We all need to have regular, consistent, disciplined sessions where we are alone. Without them, we are missing out on a powerful aspect of spiritual formation. In these quiet times, God can speak to us. This can happen as we read God's word, journal or simply listen for his voice. Some different things you may want to do during times of quiet are:

■ Take a walk in nature and ask God to reveal himself in his creation.
■ Sit for thirty minutes completely still and meditate on the character of God.
■ Find a quiet place and read through one of the gospels.
■ Journal and tell God how much you love him in writing.

The key is silence. We live in a busy and loud culture. Take time to seek silence.

prayer exercise:

Take some time to be alone with the Father. Ask God to speak to you, and tell him that you make room in your life for him. Then sit for several minutes in silence and listen for God's voice. At the end of your time, take out your schedule or day-timer and mark off an extended time where you can be alone with God this week. Ask God to make you a person who looks forward to time alone with him.

DISMANTLED: FEAR OF BEING ALONE

not good
for man to be alone

Dan was a guy who loved God and enjoyed life. He had a great time in high school and college hanging out with friends and sharing his life with them. After Dan graduated from college, he decided to go to graduate school to study marketing. He dreamed of owning a marketing firm and making lots of money. Dan was from the West Coast, but he got into one of the best marketing schools in the country in Boston. When he arrived at school, he threw himself into his studies. The first two weeks were a whirlwind, and he did not have much time to think. But as he started to settle into his new routine, Dan realized he was extremely lonely. He hadn't met anyone at school worth hanging out with, and he missed hanging out with his friends from high school and college. He tried to keep in touch with them through phone calls and e-mails, but it wasn't the same. As time went on, Dan got pretty depressed. He was miserable.

Lying in bed one Saturday night, Dan cried out to God, "Father, I can't do this anymore. I feel so alone. Please help me." The next morning, he woke up early and decided to go to a church one of his teachers had recommended. It turned out to be a great decision. That morning he met two guys in a similar situation, and they began spending time together. Over the next two years, Dan built the strongest friendships he had ever had. God showed him the power in community. Dan learned that it is definitely not good for man to be alone.

■ Have you ever been in a situation similar to Dan's?

   ❏ yes
   ❏ no

Explain that situation.

_____

_____

_____

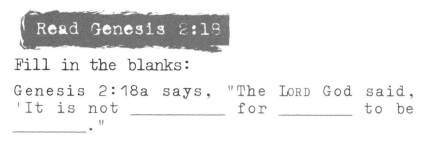

Fill in the blanks:

Genesis 2:18a says, "The LORD God said, 'It is not _____ for _____ to be _____.'"

Yesterday, we talked about the importance of spending time alone with God. But while we need regular times alone with God, we also need other people around us. This verse shows us that community was God's idea. He was the one who said it was not good for someone to be alone. God said that for a reason. He never intended for us to walk through life alone. Part of his good creation was putting Adam and Eve together.

God loves it when we worship him in a community of believers. This is the way he designed life to work. God is the author of life and the author of community. When you find yourself wanting to experience deep relationships with other people, know that desire comes from the Father. Remember that God himself is community: God the Father, God the Son, and God the Holy Spirit. Community comes from God.

■ What is your definition of community?

_____

_____

■ Are you currently walking with a community of believers?

❑ yes
❑ no

If so, what does that community look like? If not, how can you begin to seek out community?

_____

_____

_____

■ What are the benefits of journeying through life with a group of people?

_____

_____

_____

_____

prayer exercise:

Thank the Father for teaching us the importance of community. Ask him to show you how to walk in community as he intends you to. Is there someone in your life you know you should reach out to right now? Is there someone who is lonely and looking for a friend? Ask God to show you how to extend community to that person. Ask the Holy Spirit to guide you into all truth concerning the power of community.

why church
is important

■ Why do you go to church? Be honest about your answer.

_____

_____

_____

_____

■ Why do you think it is a big deal for Christians to meet together regularly?

_____

_____

_____

_____

Growing up, I never knew why I went to church every Sunday and Wednesday. My parents made me, so I just did it. As I came up through my youth group, I loved hanging out with friends and fellowshiping together. But if you had asked me why I went to church, I don't know what I would have said. It wasn't until I was 24 that God showed me the importance of the community of the church.

One of my seminary professors, Dr. Robert Smith Jr., preferred small classes to big ones. Dr. Smith is the best teacher I ever had, and some of my classes with him had only ten to twelve people in them. After class, we spent another couple of hours talking and praying through what we had experienced in the classroom. One day, as we laughed and celebrated together, a powerful thought came to my mind. I realized that these meetings were what church is really about. I started reading through the book of Acts, and God began to show me the power in community. We were never meant to walk through life alone.

It was during that time in seminary that I began to take the idea of meeting together seriously. Attending church took on a different meaning for me. I loved being with other believers and walking through life with them. I wish I had learned this truth at an earlier age. Just because you go to church does not mean that you are walking in community. Community is having a group of people close to you with whom you do life. That's what church is supposed to be like. When I discovered that blessing, it changed my life.

Read Hebrews 10:19-25

Fill in the blanks:
Hebrews 10:25 says, "Let us not give up _____ _____, as some are in the habit of doing, but let us _____ one another—and all the more as you see the Day approaching."

■ Why does the author of Hebrews say that we should not give up meeting together?

_____

_____

_____

Believers in the early church went through a lot of persecution that many of us would have a hard time even imagining today. They were beaten and killed for what they believed. But despite those obstacles, Christianity grew in many different areas, and people came out from under the slavery of the law to the freedom in Christ. New believers learned more and more each day. In order to grow in their faith, Christians had to meet, study, pray, wait, listen, and hang out together. If community was important for them then, it is important for us as well. There is power in community. When believers meet together, Jesus is in their midst. I don't believe God takes church meetings casually. The Bible makes it clear that God believes in the power of the community of the church.

God shows us many things about himself as we walk through life with others in community. We learn to be open and honest as we share our lives with others. We learn to put the needs of others above our own selfish needs. God commands us to meet together regularly. That's what the church is designed for. We must be careful to avoid the trap of being involved in many things but not truly knowing anyone. God wants us to be in community so that we can be real and authentic before others and before him.

■   Are you currently involved in a community of believers at your church?

    ❏ yes
    ❏ no

If you answered "yes," describe how community has benefited your spiritual formation. If you answered "no," list some things you can do to find an authentic community to with which to journey.

_____

_____

_____

_____

_____

Take some time to ask the Holy Spirit to show you the importance of community. You may want to read the book of Acts and look at the role community played in the early church. Focus today on Acts 2-4. Ask the Lord how you can experience a similar kind of tight-knit community with other believers. Thank him for the gift of community.

a whisper in the cave

Have you ever been caving—or spelunking, as the experts call it? About a year ago, I got my first taste of this spine-tingling experience. (Let's just say I still call it caving.) I was speaking at a camp in West Virginia that prided itself on extreme activities. It was the kind of camp kids love but one that would scare adults to death. Our week there was filled with mountain climbing, rappelling, whitewater rafting, and—of course—caving. I'm a bit of an extreme-sport enthusiast, so I was actually looking forward to caving, because I had never done it before. I even went to the guides and asked them to lead us on the most thrilling route. Then I got into the middle of a cave.

When I pictured caving, I pictured walking through the mountains, walking into a cave, turning on some flashlights, looking around, seeing a bat or two, and leaving. I thought that the bats would be the scariest part of the cave. But not too long into my caving experience, I realized I was wrong. The scariest thing about caving is the cave. Before I knew it, I was face down in mud crawling and shimmying on my stomach through something our guides called the whisper crawl. I thought I was going to die. Here's a tip: just about the worst time to discover that you're claustrophobic is when you're face down in mud in a cave. I learned that the hard way.

We went on seemingly endless crawls with grown adults like me making their way through spaces an 8-year-old could barely fit through. Imagine crawling under a kitchen chair for 40 yards at a time with someone's feet in your face and someone's face at your heels. You can't turn around, and you can't go forward unless the person in front of you goes. You're basically trapped the whole time.

We even went on one crawl through a space called the birth canal. I should have known better than to try this just based on the area's name. This crawl was so tight you could only go through sideways. I'm still not sure how I made it out of there. One of the most memorable times of the whole trip was when the worship leader lost his pants on the way through.

I thought all that was hard, but probably the most excruciating part of the entire journey came when our guide challenged us to go on about a thirty-five-yard crawl in silence with the lights on our helmets turned off.

The only communication we had came when we touched the person in front of or behind us. I did OK at first, but then the guide put me last in line, and I became separated from the group for a moment. When that happened, thoughts of water rushing through the cave or getting lost or getting stuck raced through my mind. I tried to compose myself, thinking that if the fourteen-year-old girls in front of me could handle this, I should be able to. But my fear got the best of me, and I screamed, probably losing the respect of the kids I was with in the process. I wanted light, and I wanted someone to reassure me that I wasn't alone.

Today, we rejoin Elijah where we left him a few days ago. He wasn't spelunking, but he was in a cave, and he experienced a lot of the same emotions we've been talking about. He wanted to know he was not alone.

Read 1 Kings 19:10-18

■ How did God speak to Elijah in this passage?
   ❑ wind
   ❑ earthquake
   ❑ fire
   ❑ whisper

■ Why do you think that it was important for God to speak to Elijah this way?

_____

_____

_____

■ What was God's message to Elijah?

_____

_____

_____

Fill in the blanks:
First Kings 19:18 says, "Yet I reserve
_____ _____ in Israel all whose
_____ have not _____ down to
_____ and all whose _____ have not
_____ him."

I spent many years of my life with the Elijah syndrome. I was so scared following God meant being alone all the time that I rarely did anything that demonstrated a passion for God. But things changed when God took my eyes off of me and helped me see his work across the world. In college, God showed me what true community looked like. On a mission trip, God reminded me that although sometimes I felt alone, people all over the world are living for him. God turned my light on and assured me I was not alone. God met me in my cave just like he met Elijah, and he whispered, "You are not alone." Today God whispers that truth to you.

prayer exercise:

If you have a map of the world that you can write or mark on, highlight or put a tack everywhere you know a Christian. If you don't have a map you can use that way, make a list of the cities and countries where people you know are serving God. Know that God is working in all these places through people like you. Then pick five of these places and pray for the people there who may be feeling alone or feeling that they are the only ones serving God. Allow God to minister to your fear as you think of others and pray for them.

_____

_____

_____

_____

_____

_____

_____

_____

_____

_____

_____

_____

_____

This page is designed to give you space to take notes during your "Dismantled" group session or to journal your reflections on the highlights of this week's study.

DISMANTLED

FEAR OF BEING UNLOVABLE

hagar:
pursued by God

face to face
with being unlovable

There are a few things that go into every movie love story: a pretty girl, an attractive guy, something that keeps them apart for most of the movie, and a happy ending. Everybody expects these things in a love story, and when they are there, we go away happy.

There's another character common to a lot of love stories: The leading man's buddy. While the buddy isn't a main character, he's usually pretty important to the plot of the movie. He encourages the leading man to go after the girl and maybe even comes up with some kind of crazy scheme to get the two people who are perfect for each other together. Most of the time, this character is the comic relief. He cracks jokes from the sidelines and gives us all a good laugh. But we know the buddy is not going to get the girl. He's not supposed to. Everybody likes the buddy, but nobody wants to fall in love with him.

If you stop and think about it, it would be hard to be an actor who always played the buddy and never got to be the leading man. It's even harder to play the buddy in real life, but that's the way some of us feel. We wonder, "Am I that unlovable?"

Read Genesis 16:1-6

Hagar wasn't the leading lady in this story. But like the buddy in a love story, she was a big part of the plot. Hagar was Sarai's maidservant, which meant she spent a lot of time with her. Although Hagar was technically a slave, she was almost as close as a member of the family. She spent a lot of time serving Sarai and was Sarai's friend.

Maidservants in that day were so close to family that, when someone's wife couldn't have children, the maidservant would take the wife's place. That's what happened here. God had promised Abram that he would be the father of a great nation (as we studied a few weeks ago), but he and Sarai were old and still had no children. So Sarai came up with the plan for Hagar to have Abram's child in her place.

That's exactly what happened, but trouble ensued. Hagar "despised" Sarai, and Sarai got so jealous she demanded that Hagar be thrown out. Abram agreed with Sarai, and Sarai treated Hagar so badly that Hagar had no choice but to flee.

Imagine how Hagar felt. She had no job, home, money, or future. Sarai, one of the closest people to her, had turned on her. Abram, the father of the child she was carrying, agreed to have her banished. Hagar was face to face with the fear of being unlovable.

■ Why is it important for us to be loved?

_____

_____

_____

_____

■ Where does the desire to be loved come from?
   ❑ Satan
   ❑ our inadequacies
   ❑ our culture
   ❑ peer pressure
   ❑ God

■ Do you struggle with the fear of being unlovable?
   ❑ yes
   ❑ no

If so, how so?

_____

_____

_____

_____

We all want to be loved. We studied this earlier as we talked about Moses and the fear of rejection. God created us with a need to be loved. But that need sometimes leads us to the fear of being unlovable. At our core, we know how flawed we are, and we wonder how anyone could love us. We think some of the same things Hagar must have thought out in the desert. We go through painful, miserable times like the one she experienced. But God meets us in this fear. That's what we'll study this week.

prayer exercise:

Be honest with God about your fear of being unlovable. Tell him about the pain you have experienced in times you were unloved. Trust that he listens to your cry and understands your hurt. Ask him to show you this week how much he loves you.

day two

when it seems
God has let you down

Exodus
2:23-25

■ Have you ever felt as though God let you down?

☐ yes
☐ no

If so, describe a situation when you felt this way.

_____

_____

_____

_____

■ How did that situation make you feel?

_____

_____

_____

_____

My freshman year in college was one of the most difficult times of my life. I felt alone, and I was as scared as I had ever been. I was away from home for the first time, and it threw me for a loop. There were no home-cooked meals, and nobody was there to encourage me at the end of the day. I remember spending many nights crying and wondering where God was. I wondered if he had turned his back on me.

One morning as I was walking to the cafeteria for breakfast, everything hit me, and it felt like my life came tumbling down. I felt as though God did not care about me anymore. He was not answering any of my prayers. There was no reprieve from the pain I was in. I cried out to God, but nothing happened. But that morning, I made a decision to trust God no matter what. Over the next few months, my pain lifted, and I slowly but surely felt God bringing me back into his embrace. I remember sitting on my bed a few months later and praying, "Thank you, Father. You are faithful."

Read Exodus 2:23-25

God chose the people of Israel as his people and promised to bless them. Israel was a small nation, but God did mighty things with them as recorded throughout the Bible. But despite God's history of faithfulness and his promises of blessing, Israel often doubted him. In this passage, the Israelites were enslaved in Egypt. They were oppressed and miserable, and, even more, they were terrified of the thought that God had abandoned them. Notice the strong language describing how the Israelites cried out to God.

Fill in the blanks:

Exodus 2:23 says, "During that _____ period, the king of Egypt died. The Israelites _____ in their _____ and _____out, and their _____ for _____ because of their _____ went up to God."

These people felt as though God had taken his eyes off of them. They were scared, depressed, anxious, and miserable. In short, they felt unlovable, and they wondered where God was.

Fill in the blanks:

Exodus 2:25 says, "So God _____ on the Israelites and was _____about them."

■ What does this verse say God was doing when the Israelites felt forgotten?

_____

_____

_____

Sometimes God allows those of us who are his people to go through painful and lonely periods. During these times, we feel as though he has turned his back on us, that he doesn't love us anymore. We have to choose between the enemy's lie and the truth in these situations.

■ **The Lie:** God does not love me anymore. He has turned His back on me.

■ **The Truth:** Even though I feel unloved and feel like God has turned his back on me, by faith I believe he has me in the palm of his hand and is forming me to be the person he wants me to be. God loves me.

We have to hold onto the truth that, no matter what our circumstances, God does not turn his back on us. In hard times, he continues to mold us into the kind of people he wants us to be. I pray that you will choose to trust the truth instead of believing the lie.

prayer exercise:

Use the space below and on the next page to write a letter to God. Talk to God about what you've learned in this passage of Scripture. Honestly express to the Father how you feel, like the Israelites did. If you feel like God has turned his back on you, talk to him about that. At the end, thank God that he looks on you and is concerned about you. Ask him to remind you of this truth even in the midst of your problems.

Jesus proves
God's love for us

John 15:9-13

As I shared yesterday, one of the biggest questions I struggle with is whether God really loves me. Some seasons are better than others. Recently, I went through a season where I wasn't sure what God was doing in my life. It was a painful time. In the midst of that struggle, God sent a friend my way. He's a guy I have known for quite a while, but we had never really built a strong friendship. We had lunch one day, and as I shared about my struggles, he lit up like a Christmas tree, because he had been exactly where I was. It was awesome to talk to someone who understood my situation.

Over the next month or so, we talked about our lives and experiences. We eventually decided to become prayer partners. This has been a blessing in both of our lives. In the middle of my battles with the fear of being unlovable, my friend was there. He still is there, praying for me, calling me, affirming me, and reminding me that God loves me and cares for me. We pray for each other and talk at least once a week. Sometimes my friend jumps in and helps me deal with things, and sometimes I jump in and help him. We are dedicated to praying for each other. By showing me love, my prayer partner reminds me of God's love for me.

Read John 15:9-13

Fill in the blanks:

John 15:9-13 says, "As the Father has _____ me, so have I _____ you. Now remain in my _____. If you obey my commands, you will remain in my _____, just as I have obeyed my Father's commands and remain in his _____. I have told you this so that my _____ may be in you and that your _____ may be complete. My command is this: _____ each other as I have _____ you. Greater _____ has no one than this, that he lay down his life for his _____."

When you read this passage, it's a wonder that any of us fear that we are unlovable. The word love fills this passage as Jesus talked about how he feels about us. And Jesus' love wasn't just words. He gave his life for us because he loves us. Jesus is the supreme example of love, and he reminds us of what God really thinks about us.

■ How hard is it for you to imagine laying down your life for someone else?

_____

_____

_____

_____

■ What does the fact that Jesus did this for us say about his love for us?

_____

_____

_____

_____

If you want to get to know God the Father, look at Jesus. Many people have a distorted picture of God because the word Father is filled with past hurts or abandonment. When we start to have such a distorted picture, we need to look at Jesus. Friends like my prayer partner help us to do that even more clearly. Jesus is the perfect expression of love, and he proves that God loves us.

■ Is there anyone who shows you the love of Christ on a consistent basis?

    ❏ yes
    ❏ no

If so, who? _____

How does that person remind you of Jesus' love?

_____

_____

_____

_____

_____

■ Do you consistently show the love of Jesus to
those around you?

❑ yes
❑ no

If so, how? If not, how can you begin to show
Christ's love?

_____

_____

_____

_____

_____

_____

prayer exercise:

Say the following prayer out loud:

Father, I give my life to you.
Please reveal the truth about your
love to me. Show me how much you
love me through your son Jesus.
Thank you for the people in my
life who remind me of that love.
Jesus, help me to be a person of
love who will love others to the
point that I would be willing to
lay down my own life for their
needs in any way you call me.
Forgive me for my selfishness, and
lead me to a better understanding
of how you see me. I love you and
pray in your name. Amen.

a reflection
of love

When I was a kid, I loved to look in the mirror. My mom and dad tell stories about how I would sit for hours in front of the mirror staring at myself and making faces. I can't tell you why I did that. It's a little embarrassing to admit I used to spend so much time admiring myself.

But the truth I've realized over the years is that I'm not alone. Many of us love to look at ourselves in the mirror. Have you ever noticed that when a person is in front of a mirror, he stands up taller, sucks in his stomach, fixes his hair and cleans out his nose? Mirrors make us do funny things as we try to make our reflection look as good as we can. When we see our reflection, it makes an impact.

■ What does the world see when it looks at the church?

_____

_____

_____

_____

■ What kind of reflection of God is the church supposed to give?

_____

_____

_____

_____

■ Do you think God is pleased when he sees the reflection of him the church gives?

❑ yes
❑ no

Explain your answer.

_____

_____

_____

Read Matthew 22:34-40

Fill in the blanks:

Matthew 22:35-40 says, "One of them, an expert in the law, tested him with this question: 'Teacher, which is the _____ commandment in the Law?' Jesus replied: '"_____ the _____ your _____ with all your _____ and with all your _____ and with all your _____." And the second is like it: "_____ your _____ as yourself." _____ the Law and the Prophets hang on these _____ commandments.'"

What reflection of God is the church supposed to give? Love. When people see the church, they should see a community that reflects the love of God. The name of the game is to love God and love people. Unfortunately, this is often not the case in churches. Today, as in Jesus' day, religious people are sometimes better known for the things they avoid and the rules they follow than for the love they show to others. When Jesus saw this legalistic attitude in the Pharisees, he told them that the greatest commandment was to love. He says the same to us.

■ Would you say your church is known for love?

　❏ yes
　❏ no

Why or why not?

_____

_____

_____

_____

■ What can you do to help your church become a better reflection of God's love?

_____

_____

_____

_____

One of the frustrating things about the fear of being unlovable is the truth that if the church were what God created it to be, people would seldom question whether they are loved. Think about this for a moment. Do you think the people in the book of Acts questioned whether God loved them? I doubt it. These early Christians shared everything they had, fellowshipped together, prayed with each other, and studied God's law in community. People who are deeply involved in the lives of other believers don't struggle as much with the fear of being unlovable. They see that God loves them through the lives of the people around them. They're living out the greatest commandment to love the Father with everything they have and to love others as well.

When we as Christians reflect God's love, we help chase away the fear of being unlovable. Through our testimony, people can see that God loves them as they are and that others love them too. May we be a group of people that reflects this love to the world.

Thank God for creating the church. Confess to him that sometimes you don't take church as seriously as you should. Ask God to forgive you for the times that you are not a reflection of his love. Ask him to show you ways to show his love to others. Praise him for his love. End your prayer by reflecting on the love God has for you.

the impossible
fear

Genesis
16:7-13

When I was growing up, my grandparents' house was my home away from home. Their huge yard was one of my favorite places to play. I had some friends who lived near my grandparents, and they came over to play all sorts of games: football, basketball, baseball, kickball, and stickball. Going to my grandparents' house was like going on vacation.

My favorite game to play in my grandparents' yard was hide and go seek. We would wait until it got dark to play so that it was scary. There were usually about five of us playing, and sometimes my grandparents even joined in. I would wear all black so no one could find me. I climbed trees, got down in ditches, hid behind a bush, or holed up in my grandparents' garage. I was great at hiding from everyone—except my grandmother. I never could outsmart her. Wherever I hid, she found me. I was always amazed when she found me. I'd ask, "How did you find me in here?" She always replied, "Because I know you."

Read Genesis 16:7-13

At the beginning of the week, we studied the story of Hagar. Our story left off with Hagar alone and pregnant in the desert, rejected by everyone close to her. Imagine being in her shoes. She must have been desperate, wondering if anyone loved her.

But something amazing happened to Hagar in the desert. God showed up. An angel met Hagar in the desert to remind her that God knew her, loved her and had not forgotten her. Hagar went from being alone and desperate to being remembered and loved. God had not rejected her. God had not forgotten her. Think about how much Hagar's emotions must have changed. Out of nowhere, God showed up and let her know she was loved.

■ List some truths you have learned this week that show you God loves you, has not rejected you, and has not forgotten you.

_____

_____

_____

_____

Hagar's story shouldn't surprise us, because the Bible is full of stories about times God showed up to love people in desert times. God loves us. He loves big and small people, black and white people, loud and quiet people, scared and courageous people, depressed and happy people, old and young people. When Hagar most needed love, God stepped in and reminded her of his love for her.

It's hard to fully grasp this story until you've been in a desert and seen God show up with his arms open wide in love. Sometimes God lets us go places where we are alone and have nowhere to run. In those times, we are terrified by the thought of moving forward. The fear of being unlovable paralyzes us. In these dark moments, though, we look up, and God is there. He reminds us that he sent his Son to die for us. He says, "My child, I know you. I love you. I have made you in my image, and I have wonderful plans for you."

■ What makes the fear of being unlovable an impossible fear?

_____

_____

_____

_____

_____

Hagar called God "the One who sees." He sees us in our darkest, most desperate moments, and he loves us in those times. The truth is that the fear of being unlovable is an impossible fear. Our Father, the One who created us, the One who sent his Son to die for us, is also the One who sees us and loves us.

prayer exercise:

Say the following prayer out loud:

Father, this really is an impossible fear, because you are love. You are full of love. You are the inventor of love. By faith, I stand on the promises of your word. I thank you for this picture of your love in the story of Hagar. I cling to this love, Lord. I accept your love for me. Help me to grow in the awareness of how much you love me. I pray this in the name of Jesus Christ my Savior. Amen.

_____

_____

_____

_____

_____

_____

_____

_____

_____

_____

_____

_____

_____

_____

This page is designed to give you space to take notes during your "Dismantled" group session or to journal your reflections on the highlights of this week's study.

DISMANTLED

FEAR OF
BEING INSIGNIFICANT

joshua:
struggling with courage

face to face
with insignificance

When I was in the seventh grade, I decided to play football. I was barely 5 feet tall and weighed next to nothing, but I loved the sport. When I reported to practice the first day, I almost fell over in fear. I was David against about fifty-five Goliaths. I remember thinking, "How in the world can I make it against all of these giants?" I remember feeling so small and insignificant.

I felt even smaller as the season went on. I was not as fast, strong, big, or mean as the other players. Two of my teammates always picked on me. I never felt like I helped the team. It didn't matter whether or not I played or was even there. I felt so useless.

■ Have you ever felt small and insignificant?

❑ yes

❑ no

Describe a particular situation when you felt this way.

_____

_____

_____

_____

■ List some people in the Bible who you think felt insignificant and briefly explain their stories.

_____

_____

_____

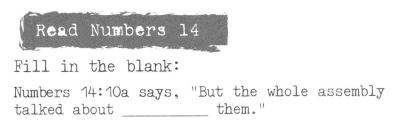

Read Numbers 14

Fill in the blank:

Numbers 14:10a says, "But the whole assembly talked about _____ them."

When God delivered the Israelites from slavery in Egypt, he led them to the Promised Land. After much wandering, the Israelites reached the edge of this land. Moses sent twelve spies to search out the land, as we saw when we looked at Numbers 13 in the first week of this Bible study. All the spies said the land was a great place to live. But while Caleb and Joshua said the Israelites could take the land with God's help, the other ten spies said there was no way to defeat the giants who lived there.

The people followed the advice of the ten spies instead of listening to Caleb and Joshua. They even wanted to stone them. Joshua had obeyed and trusted God, but the Israelites wanted to stone him.

■ How do you think Joshua felt when the people hated the news he brought back?

❑ He was angry.

❑ He didn't care.

❑ He felt like what he said didn't matter.

Joshua later took over for Moses as the leader of Israel. But he must not have felt like much of a leader. When he was a spy, the people shot down his ideas and even wanted to stone him. Joshua had come face to face with feeling small and insignificant. The people didn't listen to him, which couldn't have been great for his self-confidence. Probably, when it came time for him to lead the Israelites, Joshua looked back on this failure and rejection. God had to tell Joshua not to be afraid, perhaps because of the scars this incident left.

We wrestle with the fear of being insignificant as well. We want to make an impact in this world, but too often our big dreams far outweigh the results of our efforts. This week, we're going to look at how God reaches out to us in the midst of this fear.

Do you struggle with the fear of being insignificant? Go to the Father and discuss this with him. Be honest with him. Ask him to show you truth in the midst of this fear. Commit to looking for God as you go through this week's devotions.

why everyone
is not good at everything

1 Corinthians
12:12-20

It would be nice to be good at everything. There would never be a problem you couldn't solve. You would never need anyone's help. You would never need someone to show you how to do something. In short, you would never need anyone at all.

One of the most common mistakes we make in dealing with the fear of insignificance is thinking we have to be good at everything. Too many times, we focus on our own weaknesses and allow those weaknesses to influence our belief about what God can do through us. We feel insignificant as we compare ourselves to others and sometimes think we have to be exactly like someone else to be used by God. When we decide we don't measure up, we walk away pretty sure we will never be used by God at all.

This is the dilemma that we found Joshua in yesterday. Joshua had spoken out as a spy, and no one had followed his leadership. Now Joshua was being asked to lead the nation, a job he was pretty sure was too big for him to handle.

The truth is that we are not good at everything. In fact, there are some things we are just plain bad at. Some of us can kick a soccer ball but can't carry a tune. Others of us are great musicians but can barely turn on a computer. It should encourage us to know that we don't have to be good at everything to accomplish something. As we work together, we accomplish more than we ever could alone. That's what a **team** is all about. We don't all have the same skills or abilities. If we did, our team might not be as good as it is. We need someone who can shoot from outside. We need someone who can rebound inside. We need goalies and forwards. We need flutists and tuba players. We need salespeople and engineers. We need people with different talents working together for the same goal.

God hasn't called us to do everything by ourselves. We can take courage in knowing we only need to play our role as part of a team. We don't have to become someone else or feel insignificant because we aren't exactly like the person beside us or the person we replaced. We can find significance in knowing that God has made us exactly the way we are for a reason.

■ What does Paul compare the church to in this passage?

    ❏ an army

    ❏ an athlete

    ❏ a body

    ❏ a house

■ What does this picture tell us about significance?

_____

_____

_____

_____

■ Why is it important that everyone plays his own role and doesn't try to play someone else's?

_____

_____

_____

_____

Paul knew our tendencies toward selfishness and insignificance, so he chose the picture of a body to show us how we are supposed to function together. Can you imagine if your body was all ears? How could you see? Or imagine you were one big nose. How could you walk? Our body is composed of ears, eyes, legs, arms, appendixes, lungs, collarbones and more. The ears can't see, but they can hear. The legs can't smell, but they move us around. Each part plays a significant role.

That's the way it is with the body of Christ. God has given each of us special gifts and abilities. He hasn't given any of us every gift. We must work together. We do not need to be ashamed of our weaknesses, our failures, and our shortcomings. We do not need to be embarrassed that we don't have every gift. God has put us together as his body. When he calls us to play a specific role, we can be sure that he will equip us to fill that role for his glory.

■ Spend some time allowing the truth of today's lesson to sink in. Use your imagination to try to accomplish the following tasks. You may be able to do some of them if you think creatively. But even if you can accomplish them, think about how inefficient your body would be if it worked that way.

■ Try to smell without using your nose.
■ Try to write without using your hands.
■ Try to walk without using your legs.
■ Try to think without using your brain.

prayer exercise:

Ask God to show you what role he wants you to play today. This may not be the role you will always play, but too many times we miss our chance to serve today because we are trying to figure out our roles for tomorrow. Listen to God as he tells you how you can play your role today. Ask God to give you his eyes to see your gifts and abilities.

through
God's eyes

Matthew
16:13-20

■ Which do you struggle with most?
❑ I think too highly of myself.
❑ I think too lowly of myself.

There are many kinds of mirrors. The mirrors at workout facilities make us look better than we really are. Entire walls are covered with mirrors designed to make us look good as we watch ourselves lift weights. The problem with these mirrors is that the favorable conditions don't give us a true picture of ourselves.

Car mirrors are designed to show objects that are far away. They give a wide-angle view designed to show us everything going on behind us. But these mirrors aren't perfect either. That's why they always have a warning that says, "Objects in the mirror may be closer than they appear."

Funhouse mirrors are great. They distort our images and give us lots of laughs. Who doesn't enjoy becoming a tall, skinny person or a short, fat person in a funhouse mirror? But if we rely on funhouse mirrors to get a true picture of ourselves, we're in trouble, because those images are not representative of who we really are.

One of the most destructive forces in the world is the faulty picture most of us have of ourselves. Sadly, Christians often struggle with this as much anyone else. Some think too highly of themselves. Others think too lowly of themselves. Each of these distortions hinders us in our walk with God. An inflated self-image leads to pride. A poor self-image leads us to the fear of being insignificant. Imagine only seeing yourself through a funhouse mirror all of your life, and you will begin to sense the struggle so many Christians face.

■ What funhouse images of yourself cause you to struggle?

_____

_____

_____

_____

■ Have these images ever held you back from accomplishing God's call on your life?
   ❏ yes
   ❏ no

If you checked "yes," please describe a situation.

_____

_____

_____

_____

■ How have these images made you feel insignificant?

_____

_____

_____

What if we saw ourselves as God sees us? It would be so freeing for us to let go of our faulty pictures of ourselves and see what God sees when he looks at us. God did this with people throughout the Bible: Moses, Gideon, Joshua and just about anyone else he used greatly. God challenged his followers to go beyond their self-images and see themselves as he sees them.

Simon Peter was no exception. Throughout the Gospels, Peter was taking his foot out of his mouth and jumping from one extreme to the next. It's hard to imagine this impulsive man becoming a stable foundation for the church. But from the beginning, Jesus saw Simon Peter in a way no one else did.

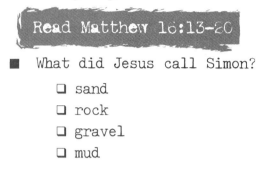

Read Matthew 16:13-20

■ What did Jesus call Simon?

❑ sand

❑ rock

❑ gravel

❑ mud

Jesus saw in Simon what Simon didn't see in himself. Jesus called him Peter, or "Rock." This must have seemed like a joke to Simon Peter's friends. But much like a master artist, Jesus saw not what Peter was but what he could become under the Savior's hand.

The same is true in our lives. As Christians, we are wrapped up in Christ. Christ is in us, and we are in Christ. So as God looks at us, he doesn't see who we are. He sees us as masterpieces into whom he has released the artistic work of his Son.

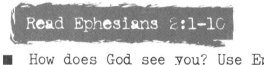

Read Ephesians 2:1-10

■ How does God see you? Use Ephesians 2:1-10 to help you journal through this answer.

_____

_____

_____

_____

_____

_____

prayer exercise:

Ask God to help you see yourself as he sees you. Read Ephesians 2:1-10 and claim the promises there. Thank God for the work he has done and is doing in you.

God
in our weakness

2 Corinthia
12:1-10

I'm not a big outdoorsman. I love eating venison but I'm not a big hunter. I don't like working in the yard very much. And I would rather take my car to a car wash than wash it by hand. However, one day my wife and I decided to wash our car the old-fashioned way. (Actually, she decided to make me wash the car.) Apart from spraying each other accidentally—yeah, right—it went pretty well. We cleaned dirt off of the car, wiped it down, rinsed it and dried it off. Certainly, we could have accomplished the same thing by taking the car to the car wash down the road and letting the machine do all the work. But I noticed some things as I washed the car by hand. I came across little dings and dents I didn't know were there and little chips in the paint that had never caught my eye before. I noticed the wear on the tires and realized I would have to replace them soon. I didn't get those insights when I drove to the car wash and came out clean on the other side.

I believe we've allowed God to wash us by hand as we've talked about the fear of being insignificant this week. We've had to come to grips with some of the chips in our paint, our dents, and our worn-out tires. We've had to admit that there are some things we aren't good at, that we can't do everything, and that most of the time we see ourselves differently than God sees us. Today, we go further to learn that God can even use the weaknesses we think hold us back to glorify him.

> Read 2 Corinthians 12:1-10

Fill in the blanks:

Second Corinthians 12:10 says, "That is why, for _____ sake, I _____ in _____, in _____, in _____, in _____, in _____. For when I am _____, then I am _____."

■ What weaknesses do you have that make you feel insignificant?

_____

_____

_____

■ How could God work through these weaknesses to make them your greatest strengths?

_____

_____

_____

The God who washed us by hand this week is also the chief tire changer, painter, and dent fixer. He specializes in our weaknesses, because in our weakness, he gains the most glory. That is why Paul could say, "I delight in weaknesses.... For when I am weak, then I am strong." That's our God. He works through people with chipped paint, dinged bodies, and worn-out tires. God uses us, weaknesses and all, to do his will. This is why Joshua could "be strong" even when he felt he was weak. And it is why, like Joshua, we can be used significantly by God. Our hope for significance is not in our strength. It is in a God so great he can even use our weaknesses to bring himself the most glory.

■ One of the greatest paradoxes of the Christian faith is that we find strength in weakness. How does that make you feel?

❑ vulnerable   ❑ happy
❑ hopeful   ❑ anxious
❑ uncomfortable   ❑ dependent
❑ mad   ❑ humble

Say the following prayer out loud.

Lord, I am weak. I know you
already know that, but it helps me
to admit it. I am chipped and
dinged and in need of your touch.
God, I need you to work in my
weaknesses. I know you specialize
in doing that. So, today I turn
my weaknesses over to you. Be
strong in my weaknesses. I know
you will be. Lord, I give you
glory. You are a good God. Amen.

DISMANTLED: FEAR OF BEING INSIGNIFICANT

the Lord
fights for you

I like to fish. I think I like it so much because growing up I spent so much time at my grandparents' house, which was on a lake. My grandfather, whom everyone called "Big Mac," taught me everything I needed to know about fishing. As soon as we pulled into my grandparents' driveway, I jumped out of the car, ran to the boathouse, and waited on Big Mac to get there.

At first, Big Mac fixed my fishing rod, baited my hook, and told me where to cast. I'd ride out in the boat with him and fish right beside him. After about an hour, I'd claim the other side of the boat as "mine" and start fishing there. But to tell you the truth, I did not do much of the fishing. Big Mac did everything. I just held the reel and did what he told me to do. I was never alone. Big Mac was there with his eye on me, guiding me to land the big one.

■ Have you ever felt God close to you, helping you walk through life?

❑ yes
❑ no

If you checked "yes," describe such a situation.

_____

_____

_____

_____

_____

_____

■ Why does the Bible put so much emphasis on abiding in Christ and walking with him?

_____

_____

_____

_____

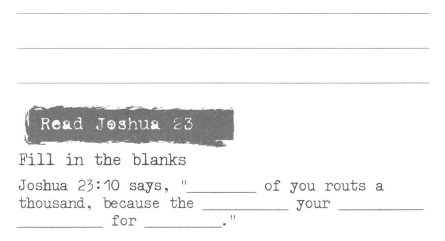

Read Joshua 23

Fill in the blanks

Joshua 23:10 says, "_____ of you routs a thousand, because the _____ your _____ _____ for _____."

The story of Joshua is one of fear, confession, and victory. When we started this week's devotional studies, we saw Joshua as a timid person who was afraid he was insignificant. But the lessons we've learned this week—why everyone is not good at everything, how God sees us, and how God uses us in our weaknesses—are some of the same lessons Joshua learned. Joshua faced his fear of being insignificant honestly before God, and by the end of his life he had seen some pretty awesome victories as God led Israel to claim the land he had promised them.

In this passage, Joshua is giving his farewell address to the Israelites, and he tells them something he learned on his journey: **Be strong!** The message that God gave Joshua over and over when he became the leader of Israel sunk in and became Joshua's rallying cry to the people. What an amazing thought. We are not alone. God is beside us with his eye on us, guiding us. And we don't even have to do the fighting. God fights for us.

■ Why do you think we tend to try to fight our battles on our own?

_____

_____

_____

■ How has God fought on your behalf?

_____

_____

_____

We leave this week with the truth that we are not small, because our big God fights for us. We are not insignificant, because God is with us. And when we are dismantled by our fears, we hang onto the truth that we don't have to fight them on our own. The Lord, in his great love, fights for us.

prayer exercise:

Take some extended time and think back over this study. Be honest with God about the fears you still face. Thank him for the ways you have experienced his love. After a few minutes, say the following prayer out loud.

Father, I love you. Thank you for having an answer to my fears. Help me to focus on you and your love for me. Help me realize that you fight for me. I trust you. In the name of Jesus I pray. Amen.

This page is designed to give you space to take notes during your "Dismantled" group session or to journal your reflections on the highlights of this week's study.

DISMANTLED
About the Authors

DAVID RHODES has a passion to guide people in the journey of the Christian faith. He speaks at camps, conferences, retreats, and churches and also writes devotional material, camp curriculum, and D-Now material. David graduated from Palm Beach Atlantic College in 1995 and earned his Master of Divinity in 2000 from Beeson Divinity School. Since 2000, David has been on staff with Wayfarer Ministries and has been a teacher at Engage, a praise-and-worship Bible study for 20-somethings in upstate  South Carolina. David's commitment to leading people to engage their hearts, souls, minds, and hands in God is evident in his preaching, teaching, and writing. David, wife Kim, and daughter Emma, live in Moore, S.C.

CHAD NORRIS desires to lead people in their journeys to become fully devoted followers of God. He does so through speaking, teaching and  writing. After graduating from the University of Georgia in 1995, Chad received his Master of Divinity from Beeson Divinity School in 2000. While at Beeson, he also served as the college minister at The Church of Brook Hills in Birmingham, Alabama. Since 2000, Chad has been on staff with Wayfarer Ministries and has been one of the teachers for Engage, a praise-and-worship Bible study for 20-somethings in upstate South Carolina. Chad's love of "the journey" and his realistic viewpoints help nurture people in their personal spiritual growth. Chad, wife Wendy, and son Samuel, live in Spartanburg, S.C.

For more information regarding the authors of this study, please contact:

Wayfarer Ministries
Box Number 201
1735 John B. White Sr. Boulevard
Suite 9
Spartanburg, SC 29301-5462
www.wayfarerministries.org

notes

notes

notes